To Cheat or Not to Cheat

Dave R. Jones

Bloomington, IN  Milton Keynes, UK

authorHOUSE

AuthorHouse™
1663 Liberty Drive, Suite 200
Bloomington, IN 47403
www.authorhouse.com
Phone: 1-800-839-8640

AuthorHouse™ UK Ltd.
500 Avebury Boulevard
Central Milton Keynes, MK9 2BE
www.authorhouse.co.uk
Phone: 08001974150

First published by AuthorHouse 3/31/2006

ISBN: 1-4259-2400-X (sc)

Printed in the United States of America
Bloomington, Indiana

This book is printed on acid-free paper.

This book is dedicated to my dad who taught me everything I know, god bless you

Roger David Jones 1954-2001

CONTENTS

INTRODUCTION

As described in the Collins English Dictionary, *cheat verb: To be sexually unfaithful to one's wife, husband, or lover.*

To be able to cheat, you must be smart, quick thinking and ready to accept that at any time you will get caught. People would not cheat if they knew that they will be found out, but accidents can happen and it will cause a lot of heartache. However, if you do get caught do not automatically assume that it is the end, because if you are smart enough you can talk your way out of anything. This book is to help you stay undetected, get out of awkward situations and what to do when it all goes wrong. It is also a guide to help you out if you think you have been cheated on, what to do, how to find out and also to read into the mind of a cheater. You may find that some of the parts may be repeated later on in the book, because they may apply to both sections of the book. Men and women all over the world cheat on their partners, and there are different reasons why this happens. I can explain what draws people to cheat. We now have to uncover what goes on inside the mind of an unfaithful partner and target the problems that trigger cheating. So lets take a good look at where it all starts...

SECTION ONE: CHEATING

PART ONE

WHO IS LIKELY TO CHEAT

To start off we have to identify what a cheat is and who is likely to cheat. The answer is simple anyone can be a cheat, they don't come in obvious clothes or are the typical baddies from films. Every person has the ability to play away from home and have a bit on the side. The only difference is that everybody deals with it in his or her own way. A lot of people accidentally cheat on their partner and have difficulty in dealing with the guilt. Others can shrug it off without showing any remorse or care about the consequences.

It all comes down to the individual. If you have been unfaithful to your partner it does not mean you are a bad person, it is not against the law but it can be against moral opinion. Some find it a way of life and others detest it in every sense, but before we condemn the person responsible for being unfaithful, we must first understand why they have done it in the first place. There are many things that can cause someone to cheat, the main reason being that the person in question is not happy in his or her relationship for whatever reason. They could feel un loved, uncared for, bored or not satisfied sexually that they feel they need to get it from other people.

The 3 points in a triangle are what make a loving couple faithful and strong. These 3 points are, happiness, love and security. If one or all of these points are broken, then the triangle will become unstable. I am not saying that this will cause someone to cheat, as most of the time the relationship will fall apart and the couple will split up. But if the person has lost any of the points in the triangle and does not want to lose their partner, then it has to be fixed or balanced out somehow. Usually by seeking it somewhere else. The person who is feeling that they are unloved, unhappy or unsecure will more than likely try to talk to their partner and tell them how they feel so that the problem can be sorted out, but on occasion the problem may fall on deaf ears or it may have been sorted out but things can fall back into the old routine. It is usually at this point when things start to happen and the cheating may begin. Here is a possible scenario, the unhappy subject may bump into an old school friend or be chatted up at a bar, club or somebody at work. It could be a case that for the first time, they are getting the attention they never receive from their partner.

Then the old phrase "one thing led to another" happens and before they know it they are doing something that they may regret in the morning.

In this scenario, the subject did not set out to cheat but it happened because he/she felt one of the missing points from the triangle had been restored, but for the wrong reasons. He/She may wake up feeling very guilty and will have to go home and face their partner. This can cause problems for some people as they feel that they have to confess the deed, while others keep it to themselves. Telling a partner that you have been unfaithful to them can break a relationship altogether, so unless you know that your relationship is strong enough to survive the truth it is advisable not to confess anything, no matter how guilty you feel. It may all be well and good telling yourself "I can't keep a secret like this, I love him/her too much." Because at the end of the day, you will end up losing everything. Its better to have a dirty secret than to have nothing at all.

Do not overestimate your current relationship on how long you have been together, what you have been through or how much they love you, it doesn't mean anything if you know in your heart that you won't be forgiven. I have been with loads of women who have all said the same thing along the lines of "I love you to bits, I will never ever leave you, we will be together forever" and its all just words. I never even take any of that seriously anymore, because sometimes it has been a case of them getting bored, meeting someone else or what ever reason may pop up. Do not be led into a false sense of security, when they say that they will never leave you, because what you don't read in the small print is, I will leave you if you screw the relationship up. Here is a Scenario to start the book off with, a man is out with all his friends and he leaves his girlfriend at home, he loves her, he has her security and he is happy, but while out he spots a beautiful blonde sitting on her own. He goes over to her, buys her a drink and chats her up. Again "one thing leads to another" he wakes up in the morning with the blonde but does not feel guilty at all, so where does the triangle come into play here if he has the love, happiness and security? Why did he cheat? It is simple, he has everything he wants, but he still wants to have more. Now this does not just happen with men, women also do this as well, it is all to do with being happy with the person you are with, but you still want to see what it is like from someone else. To see if the sex is better, or if they are better to talk to, maybe it's the case that you want to show off to your mates that you can leave a bar, club with a really nice looking person.

9 times out of 10 in this situation the man/woman who has cheated will not feel any guilt at all, because he/she may not think that they have done anything wrong, because it was planned from the start or "only a bit of fun." And in this case 1 in 10 people will feel guilty or confess to their partner. This is also the same situation where affairs from work or in general can start. The other person may know that you are married or in a relationship, and for them they can feel a bit of adventure, and it can be a turn on. However, affairs can become dangerous, because if they know you are married and they become more and more attached to you, then after a while, they can totally disregard your marriage completely and want you for themselves. For example, they may become jealous of your wife/husband and try to get you to leave him/her, if you cannot make the sacrifice, the affair can become unstable and they may resort to threatening to tell your wife/husband. As you can tell, this will cause a lot of problems, but I will explain how to deal with this later on. A cheat who has been found out will generally swear that it was a one off mistake and it will never happen again, but if the problem started from the relationship, then it is likely

to happen again unless there are significant changes made.

With this in mind, the cheat, will realise he/she has been found out and learn from their mistake so they won't make the same one again. After all we wouldn't cheat if we knew we would get found out, just like someone who breaks into a house. If that person knew that he would leave behind a vital piece of evidence that will land him in prison, he would not do the crime. Some people do however learn from their mistake and it hits them that they really do not want to lose their partner, it takes a short sharp shock to knock sense into some people. You will find that your partner who you cheated on will be very different towards you if they decide not to end the relationship. They will be very possessive, jealous and may also be very hard on you. This is natural, after all, they will be feeling very hurt and you will have a lot of making up to do. It can also be some time before you can get their trust back, if not at all. So when reading this please be aware of what you are getting yourself into and the big problems you may face if you are found out.

PART TWO:

THE BASICS & STEALTH PHONES

We have now identified some of the most obvious points on what causes people to cheat, now we will look into how to be a successful cheat. I kid you not, from experience, cheating is not easy, I have done it many times to lots of people. However the many years when I was playing 3-5 girls at a time, I learned a lot of tricks and I never got caught once.

The reason why so many people get caught out is because they do not plan ahead, and are careless. People who just jump into things without thinking or planning are ALWAYS heading for disaster. You have to be on top at all times and always have a plan ready in your head. You must be ready for any situation that may catch you out when you least expect it, because it is always when you least expect it when you get caught. Here are some examples.

1. Lover calls you when you are with your partner.
2. You bump into your partner when you are with your lover or vice versa
3. Your partners friend sees you out with your lover or vice versa

4. Your lover tells your partner you have been cheating
5. Your partner checks your bank statements, email or the phone bill
6. Your partner catches you in bed with your lover
7. You confess
8. Your partner becomes suspicious and wants answers or investigates you.

These are 8 obvious examples of being caught out. Do you think you would know what to do if you faced any of these situations? Unless you have planned ahead, then maybe not, but then I can tell you how to prevent all of these events happening in the first place so you don't have to worry about explaining yourself. The most important thing you have to be able to do is lie. If you cannot lie to save your life then, don't even bother with the cheating game, because you will not get very far. It does not matter if you have not been found out, because you still have to lie when have to explain why you aren't coming home or you have other plans, its that simple. It's a proven scientific fact that professional liars CAN beat the lie detector test. Criminals who have lied throughout their life can do it so well that they believe the lie they are telling and show no signs that the lie detector test looks for.

This is how you have to be, because when caught out with a question, you need to have your answer, fast, accurate and believable. If you stumble, stutter or look lost with the answer, then you are not going to convince anyone. If you are not used to lying then, get some practice, the best person to lie to is your mother. If you cannot lie and convince her (being as she has known you all your life and knows exactly when you are lying) then there is no way you are going to convince a suspicious partner. Phone her up and when she asks what you have been up to, then just make it up as you go along, and see how it goes. The best way to have a convincing story is to tell her a lie about something you actually have done, but not last week, because alough it's a lie, it is something you did and its something you can easily remember. Or you could tell her you did something that a friend told you he had done in the week. Tell her the story exactly how your friend told you.

It could be anything from a fishing trip to going to the cinema. Be creative, but make sure it sounds convincing. Eventually if you do this a couple of times by telling more people the same story, you actually believe you really went on the fishing trip, and soon it does not feel like you are lying. Just make sure you remember not to tell your friend about the fishing trip when he was the one that told you. This is the next thing you have to take note of. A lot of people have been caught out by lying because they forgot the lie they told. What I mean is, we always remember telling the truth, but we may forget about what we lied about. Here is an example, you want to see your mistress so you tell your girlfriend that on Tuesday night you are going to the pub with Bill from down the road. A week later you say to your girlfriend "I fancy going to see Bill I haven't seen him for months." She will obviously say, "I thought you went out with him last Tuesday." You have forgotten the lie you told her last week and say "No. When did

I say that?" Now you have put your foot in it because you completely forgot that you used Bill as a cover and she will become very suspicious and say "Well if you weren't with Bill on Tuesday, then where were you?" If it gets to this stage then you must realise what happened on Tuesday and it could be too late, especially if you came home the Tuesday night and told your girlfriend all about what you and Bill got up to.

So all I can say is try and keep a secret diary of when you go out and what you have told your girlfriend/ boyfriend, because remembering can save your skin. Especially if you could have said something like "I did go to the pub on Tuesday, but Bill didn't turn up, that's why I said I haven't seen him for months." Being caught out with your own lie can be very embarrassing, especially if it was something so simple. Hopefully this will help you out a bit, because you cannot cheat without lying, and good liars get away with so much more.

It is also advisable that you do not tell your friends you have a secret lover, as this may count against you in the future. Because if they do not know then they won't accidentally drop you in it or say you where somewhere else when you told your partner you were with them. Not to mention if you have an argument with your friends then they could just end up telling your partner you play away. However having one or two select friends know about your affairs can be useful if you need an emergency alibi, however I recommend that you only keep it to a minimum few people. You must have the confidence that they will never drop you in it and that they know everything they need to in an emergency if you need them to confirm your whereabouts. I knew someone who got caught out because his girlfriend was suspicious he was cheating on her, and she phoned up one of his friends and said that he had confessed everything to her and she just wanted to know how long he had been cheating for. Naturally the friend who knew about it said something like, only about 3 months. So the girlfriend had tricked the friend in getting a confession. So its always good to tell your friends that only you will tell them if you have told your partner and this will prevent any confusion if the partner calls them pretending to know everything.

You can use friends for cover or get them to tell your partner that you were with them when you were with someone else, especially if you have discussed with them what they need to say in an emergency. For instance, you may have been caught out, you can say "I was with Bill all last night, if you don't believe me then phone him up and ask him." Hopefully you will have spoken to Bill before hand and told him what to say if your partner ever phoned him up to verify your story. Just be sure that both of your stories match, because having an alibi is no good if you say you were at his house all night and Bill says you were both at the pub all night. If you decide to tell your friends I would also suggest that they are closer to you than your partner, because they may not approve, especially if your friend happens to be your partners brother. This is a big mistake, because the last thing he wants is to see his little sis hurt by you cheating on her. Its usually best to tell friends your partner does not get on with because they won't question what you got up to or want to call them to verify your story.

In all cases of cheating you will at some stage come close to being found out or questioned on your whereabouts or a suspicion your partner may have, it is just the way it is.

You have to make sure you are prepared. It all comes down to the old army 6 P's, which stands for, "proper prior preparation prevents poor performance." You must not jump into anything without first thinking through all the possible outcomes. You must have a cover story for everything you do and be ready for any situation that may happen. So sit down and think about what to do in an emergency. What you will say if this happens, what you will say if that happens, because in the end if you have your story all planned out then you won't have trouble finding words to say or stumble on a lie that won't work.

People will buy lies that come straight out without you pausing to think of something, because in their mind they are thinking, "well he must be telling the truth because he didn't have much time to think that story up." Here is another problem that many people overlook, it is perfectly fine being confident in telling lies, but you can give it away so easily with your body language. Your body is an easy lie detector tool if you know what signs to look for. The police and government agents like the FBI, CIA, MI5 etc… are trained to look for body language when it comes to liars. There are 14 points on a man that will give you away, and a woman has 19 points. Most are not even aware of the fact that they are signalling a lie it is all a subconscious thing. If you are not careful your body will tell the truth. First of all if someone asks you a question that you do not know or have to think of, you will look up, if you are lying you will look down. These are the most obvious signs people do when they are nervous and have to lie to save their skin.

It is always better to look the person in the eye and do not look away, this can be hard but it is the safest way to answer a question. The other signs are when people cannot sit still. You may fidget or play with your hands or hair. This is because you feel uncomfortable and are having trouble dealing with the situation. You must sit perfectly still and do not show any signs of stress. A common mistake people make is to continuously scratch their nose. This telltale sign is caused by a high blood pressure of the heart beating faster because of stress and the small blood vessels in the nose become irritated which cases you to scratch them. Or if you don't scratch your nose you may flair your nostrils which can be an uncontrollable muscle spasm, and also quite obvious. Many people do not know this but to seek out a liar is in the eyes, if you are lying your pupils will dilate and this can happen mostly when you are nervous.

The small muscles above your eyes may spasm or twitch, and give you away.

Vomiting can be caused by feelings of strong guilt. Some people can feel so guilty that they are unable to control this from happening.

I have demonstrated some of the most obvious signs of a liar, you have to be confident on your story, so confident that you do not get nervous and you are able to remain cool all the time. Your heart rate will beat faster revealing a lot of the visible signs, mentioned like the itchy nose or the dilated pupils, but also a fast heartbeat may cause you to sweat. This is why I said try practicing lying to people so you can get good at it, Try and tell a lie and deliberately get caught out, see how well you are at recovering yourself, and after a while with practice you will not give away any signs from your body. Now lets try and see how to prevent some of the most obvious accidents from happening.

I found out this little trick very quickly when I nearly got caught out myself, but imagine this scenario: You are sitting at home with your partner, and then suddenly, out of nowhere, you get a text or phone call from your secret lover. Would you A. answer it? No, big mistake, you are going to go down like the Titanic. Or would you choose answer B. Don't answer it? No another mistake, if you don't answer it then your partner is going to wonder why. You can say it's a private number and you don't answer private numbers, but if you are with a possessive or jealous person, he/she may want to have a look at your phone to see if you are telling the truth and it can be a hard thing to hide.

Especially when they say "If you haven't done anything wrong then you have nothing to hide." This can be a hard situation to get out of, unless you have already thought ahead. There may be a time when your secret lover may phone you up when you are with your partner. So how do you stop this from happening? Its very simple, It's answer C. you get yourself a "stealth" phone. No I am not talking about a bomber that is undetectable to radar, but a normal mobile phone that is undetectable to your partner. Having 2 phones is the safest way to lead a double life. Buy a cheap one from Ebay and also get a pay as you go sim card. The reason why you have to get a pay as you go card is because you do not get a monthly bill and your partner will not see you paying the bill with your bank if you get the top up cards from a shop.

This way you can now sit comfortably with your partner without worrying about getting a phone call at the wrong moment. There is a simple rule that I always stuck to and that was if I were round my girlfriends my stealth phone would be hidden at home and switched off. If you are living with your partner you must have somewhere good to hide it so they will never find it, because it is no good having a stealth phone if your partner finds it or knows you have it. This also applies when you go to see your lover, only take your stealth phone with you, and do not put your partners number on the phone.

This is because if you are with your lover and you have to leave the room to use the toilet or something, they may go through it and find your partners number and will want answers. Not to mention if you have your normal phone with you, then you won't want them adding it to their phone book because it will defeat the object of having a stealth phone if they are still going to call and text you anyway. Also you won't text or call your partner from your stealth phone by accident if you do not store them in the phone book. Now this is a problem that may arise when you have finally got away from your partner and you turn on your stealth phone. You have about 12 missed calls and 8 texts asking why your phone is off or why you haven't replied to any texts in 2 days.

This can be quite simple to explain if you know what you are doing. The best excuse is to say that your area has no signal and sometimes it can take days go get a single bar on your phone. A lot of people can appreciate this excuse and may not ask again. Or you could say that your phone is faulty and it wont charge properly, so you have to keep it off sometimes because it won't charge anymore than 2 battery bars. This can be an acceptable excuse with old phones, but they will end up saying something like "Why don't you get a new phone?" So it's always better to go with the signal problem. As you are on pay as you go, then you may not have credit to call or text back so this can always be a good reason. Most people who rely on credit are nearly always saying "I haven't got any credit" or "I only have a little bit left." So you shouldn't have any problems at all with this. You must make sure that only a few people know about your stealth phone, the fewer the better, don't even tell your friends about it, because it can take only 1 person to tell your partner on a drunken night out that you have it and alough he/she has to prove that you do own another phone, you do not need the hassle.

If you cannot afford a stealth phone or choose not to get one, then don't worry, there is still hope. Things will be a bit harder and you need to be a little bit more vigilant but if you know what to do then everything will be fine. The first thing to eliminate is detection, and that is, not having your lover's number in your phonebook under their real name, unless its someone your partner knows and will accept having on your phone. Change their name to anything you want so long is it is not the opposite sex or might cause questions if noticed. If you have a friend that your partner does not like or is not likely to call then put it in their name.

The next step is making sure you delete any call logs, texts or sent messages to that number. Remember, its evidence that can be used against you, and evidence is bad. I mentioned about getting a call or text at the wrong moment, obviously you cannot help getting a call, but at least with text messages you can be more discreet and easily text back while your partner is in the room, (providing they are not next to you or over your shoulder.) Would you like to know how to prevent getting texts completely? Simply tell your lover that you do not get free texts or you do not like text messages because you find them annoying. Say that there is no point texting you because you do not respond to them. In most cases this will prevent them from bothering, the only problem is it gives them more of a reason to call you. So if your phone keeps ringing and you don't answer it then it may arise suspicion. Not unless you turn off the vibration and keep it on silent. When you are asked why you don't answer the phone by your lover, then you can say that there is no signal and you did not receive a call. Not having a stealth phone and keeping it on silent is risky, so you must always keep your phone on you at all times and do not leave it lying around. If you are in the shower and your partner notices that you have a missed call they might check to see who it is and call them back.

PART THREE

How Not To Get Caught

The most obvious reasons for getting caught is carelessness. You are the only person that will let yourself down if you get caught because you did not cover your tracks properly or you were found in your own bed with another person. I have no pity for people that cry after they have been caught because they only have themselves to blame. I wouldn't have written this book if I had been caught in my past, because I couldn't have been a good enough cheat to get away with it. I have given tips out to many of my friends on how to cheat and it has always been a success, and I have always been there for them if their partners have left them or cheated on them too. I have a good way with people and I usually know what to say to make them feel better if they have just lost the love of their life, I do believe that two wrongs don't make a right so if I found out that my ex girlfriend had cheated on me, I would not find it in my heart to shout and scream at her because I would be a hypocrite. Yes I would feel hurt and upset, but then what goes around comes around. I will explain later on in this book what to do if you have been cheated on or if you want to find out if your partner is cheating on you, but first, lets look at how to stay undetected. First you must have your stealth phone, that is one thing that will prevent you from being caught, I do not see anything else I need to cover with the stealth phone, so lets look at how to prevent getting caught out in person.

The number one rule is never to shit on your own doorstop.

This is extremely dangerous and you are very likely to get caught one way or another. The best way to have a secret lover is to have one that does not live in the same town as you or your partner. It is an added bonus if they cannot drive because this means that you can only see them if you go to visit them at their house. You do not really want them to know where you live or where you are likely to stay when you are with your partner, because you will not be prepared if they plan to make a surprise visit to your house when you are cuddled up to your partner. You should always go and see them or if you have a friend that lets you stay at his house, you can take them there instead, so long as you have an understanding with your friend that they know the situation.

You do not want to be seen out in public with your lover if it is in the same town as where you or your partner lives, because this is just asking for trouble. Anyone can see you walking down the street holding hands, and that anyone could be your partner or any of your partner's friends. This carelessness is stupid and unforgivable, do not even attempt it. Feel free to walk along arm in arm with your lover in their town because if it is a fair distance away from you, then its pretty safe that nobody will spot you out. If you have a favourite place or bar that you take your partner to, again it is not advisable to take your lover to the same spot, because your partner may recommend the place to their friends and family, and you will only be walking into a courtroom with the judge and jury waiting to hang you. Even the locals who you probably don't talk to will notice if one night you come in with one lover and a different one on another night, words may be said and you will be caught out. So take note of the risks because they just are not worth it. In some cases, it might be advisable not to be seen in public at all, regardless of which town you are in. This is very unlikely to happen, but it DOES happen, and that is if your partner becomes suspicious, they may find it necessary to call in a private investigator or a friend to follow you and see what you get up to. If you are videoed or photographed walking in public, hand in hand with another person, then you have nothing in your defence that can explain it. I am a fully qualified Private Investigator, and have a diploma so I know that they have excellent training in surveillance and tracking people down. Most people do not even know they are being watched, so you have to be aware of everybody around you. If you choose to cheat in public, watch your back, because you do not know who is following you. Private investigators do not look like agents from the Matrix films, nor do they walk around with big brown trench coats, hats and dark glasses. They look just like every other person walking past you in the street.

Most people do have a sixth sense that they are being watched. It is a psychic subconscious feeling that we cannot explain. However, if you feel that you are being followed or watched, then do not leave it to chance, try to make sure that you are not doing anything that can be used against you. This could be anything from stop holding hands, or saying quietly that you need to go to another shop and you will meet up in a minute.

See who is around you, walk away, and check again. If you see someone who you saw 5 minutes ago following you, then it could be someone checking up on you. Go home, even if it means you abandon your lover in a shop. You can easily say that you had a phone call from the hospital saying that your mother had been taken in from a heart attack. Being left in a shop without warning can be very distressing, but understandable in the right circumstances.

If you think that you have been followed for a little while, then try to see if the same faces keep appearing, like I said before, try to be aware of everyone around you. Obviously if you are being followed, then somebody has arranged it. Check your phone bill for any unusual numbers, see if you can get hold of your partners mobile phone and check that. If there is a number that looks out of place, then check it up in the yellow pages or Internet directory. It could match that of a private eye firm. If this is confirmed then you will have to try and remember where you have been for the last couple of weeks and when you first felt that you were being watched. From this point on, make sure that you do not put yourself in any compromising situation. You do not know how long you have been put under surveillance or how long it will go on for, so your only course of action now is to carry on with your life innocently. The advantage with private detectives is that they can be quite costly, and most are put off from using them. It does not stop people from using their friends or doing it themselves, so don't assume that it won't happen.

When somebody mentions a private investigator, nearly all people come to the same conclusion. Most think private investigators only do one kind of job, and if you ask anyone what a private investigator is, every time you will get this answer, "They follow cheating husbands around." So with this in mind, how many people do you think have been followed by a PI for them to get this reputation? As you can see I have now explained the dangers of cheating in the same town and the same places you normally visit with your partner, so does this include having sex in your own house? Well yes it does, I mentioned above that you must not bring a lover to your own house because knowing too much about you and your life can be devastating.

You do not want to be entertaining your lover and have your partner ring the house phone or to turn up at your front door. It is near to impossible to turn away your partner if they arrive at your house, so do not take the risk. This is the same if your partner is living with you and he/she has to go out for the night, or weekend because you cannot guarantee they will not come home early. Even if they say they are at their mothers for the weekend, how do you know if they have an argument with their parents and come home early? Like I have said, no matter how sure you are that your partner will be away, there could always be something that can happen where they come home sooner than expected. Being found in bed with another person by your husband or wife, is the worst thing that can happen, there is absolutely nothing you can do to talk your way out of it and you will lose both your partner and your lover, (unless they already know that you are attached.) A problem that may arise if your lover starts asking you why you never take them to your house can get you stuck for answers.

If you have a friends house to take them to then that is okay, but if not, you can always say that your house is a complete mess or you are sharing with other people and you won't get the chance to have peace and quiet together. More often than not these excuses will always work, but they won't work for too long so try and think of a reason why you don't want to bring them home. Just remember to be convincing with your story.

You may think that you are very careful in covering your tracks but just exactly how careful are you? Remember that any link you have with your lover will create a trail behind you so make sure that you do not leave any evidence. This can be anything from forgetting to put your stealth phone away to having sexy underwear left on the back seat of your car. You also need to make sure that you do not have any evidence on your computer about your lover. Make sure you have deleted any email messages sent and received, this is critical if others use your pc. Even if you have been sent an email that you think is too nice to delete, then make sure you print it out and hide it. This is another thing many people overlook, because emails can contain details of all your sordid adventures and you will have a lot of trouble trying to talk your way out of it, so it's always better to make sure you don't need to face an interrogation by covering up any evidence.

Do not even store their email address on your computer, as deleting the evidence is no good if you keep the source. If you use internet dating websites then make sure you have different passwords and do not use your own email address registered with the site, I will explain why later. Make sure you delete all your history and cookies in your Internet options. If you do email your lover, write their details down on a piece of paper and do not store them in your address book. Wedding and engagement rings are also considered evidence as well, so be sure to remove them when going to see your lover. Here is a clever trick I learned, but it is a hard one to keep going, especially as you need to have a good memory and its even harder if you want your friends to stick to it as well.

You can try and have a secret lover by pretending to be a sort of secret agent, I don't mean like James Bond, but you can pretend to be someone completely different from yourself. It is a safe way to cheat, but hard because you need to keep track of everything you have said and done. By giving a fake name, a fake job a fake address and a fake life.

Why say you are a builder when you can try and impress them by saying you work as a rocket scientist. You have to be careful though, because you may have spent weeks making up this character that your lover thinks you are, and it will all go to pot if you answer the phone and you end up saying, "sorry you got the wrong number" or one of your friends calls you your real name in front of them. It may sound childish, but there is a good reason for doing it. Firstly, if your lover somehow gets your real home phone number and your partner answers, then your lover will only know you by a different name, so when they ask for you, your partner will tell them that they have the wrong number.

If you use your real name then you may have some explaining to do when your partner asks who was on the phone. This is the same if your partner finds your lover's number and wants to find out if you have been cheating. Your partner could say something like "Have you been sleeping with my husband? His name is John Smith and he lives with me at 55 Walkern road?" The lover will probably answer with "No, I have a boyfriend called Peter Harris and he lives at 21 Pond Lane." This will eliminate you right away, you just have to hope that they do not give a description of what you look like because this will give you away. Having another identity can be very hard to keep up as your real name will be on your cards in your wallet, your friends you may bump into you and call you by your real name and you might subconsciously slip up in conversation and say your real name so trying to have an alternate identity is fun but only for those who are confident they can keep it up.

There is a type of relationship that you need to be careful of, and that is a possessive one. I used to have an ex girlfriend who was very possessive and jealous of me, so how do you think I managed to get away with having 3-5 other girlfriends and also have time to work and sleep? I can tell you that my life was very well planned out and extremely hectic. My main girlfriend wanted me to be with her all the time and didn't respect my right to personal space so with this in mind I had a 48-hour per week job, to contend with. The luck was in my favour because my job required me to work, 12 hour days, nights and weekends with overtime. So I would tell my main girlfriend that I was working an overtime nightshift when I went to see one of my other girlfriends. Then I would see another one the next day during the morning and afternoon, because my main girlfriend thought I would sleep after my nightshift until half 4 in the afternoon. I would then go to see her at 5 for an hour till I was due back at work again.

On few occasions she would try to catch me out by sending me a text with delivery report so she would tell when I turned my phone on, but that didn't matter to me because my stealth phone would be on all day so if I needed to call work or my mother I would use the stealth phone. I would always plan every week as it came and have everything planned out in my diary right down to the last minute, so I could see more than one person in the same day without causing suspicion. You do not have to use work as an escape, if you have a hobby, like fishing or paintball, something that your partner has no interest in and also a hobby that won't have a phone number to contact you by.

But if you say you are going fishing then you have to make it convincing, by taking your rods with you, put them in the boot of your car and cover them up if you have to because you won't need them until you come home again.

Also If you have just slept with your lover and you are going to see another lover or your main partner, then you must make sure you have cleaned yourself up of any perfume, smells or stains that can easily be identified as semen or vaginal discharge. These can have a very obvious and potent smell and will give you away in an instant, so make sure you have a shower and spray yourself with deodorant afterwards. If you haven't had a chance to shower and you arrive home to your wife/ husband, make sure you do not make any close contact with them, jump into the bath or shower immediately and wash yourself off. A welcome home kiss and cuddle will give off any smells that have been rubbed off onto you and if have apparently been out fishing you will not be smelling of women's perfume.

The ultimate disaster can happen if you are not careful, so made sure that if you have sex with your lover you wear protection. I do not care for excuses like "She told me she was on the pill." So what if she was, that does not stop you from catching a sexually transmitted disease that you will pass on to your partner? How are you going to explain to your wife/ husband of 3 years that you have suddenly contracted HIV? You have no way of explaining it unless you have been sleeping with someone else. I have also heard enough stories of men sleeping with women that were apparently on the pill but still became pregnant. You are both in charge of the sexual relationship and the best and most effective contraception is a condom. Yes you may lose some sensation in sex but it is a small price to pay than catching an STD or getting your secret lover pregnant. I have said it enough times already and that is carelessness will eventually always catch you out, so do not take the chance. I think the only way of getting away from someone if they become pregnant is if you have adopted the alternate identity approach, because you can just disappear into thin air. And they will end up trying to track down someone you created in your head. You just have to make sure that there is nothing in your fake identity that will lead back to your real identity.

Being in a relationship with a possessive and jealous secret lover can be a problem as well especially if they do know that you are married, because these relationships have a habit of turning nasty if you split up, and the last thing you need is a bunny boiler after your blood. Having them know too much about you and your marriage can be dangerous, because if things do turn bad people who have nothing to lose are very unstable and can resort to anything that may destroy your life. So ending a relationship with a possible bunny boiler may not be the best course of action. When I used to have 3 girlfriends on the go, I made sure that I had a cover plan set up in the event that I needed to end the relationship quickly and easy. Because of my job, at the time I was required to sometimes work abroad for long periods, so when I met a new lover I would always tell her about my job at the start and that I could be called up to work in France or Germany for up to 2 years at any time.

This way they are prepared for it and it will be more believable if 6 months down the road you want to end it you can say, "I'm so upset, the company have called me up to work in France, I knew this was coming for weeks. I will be working out there for 2 years, I really don't want to go." This is one of the best ways to end a relationship, because you are telling them that you have to leave them, but you really don't want to. I think I have an old lover that still thinks I am working in France and is still waiting for me to come home.

I lost contact with her so I can't tell her to stop waiting for me, but I'm sure she has moved on. A situation like this is what I call my emergency escape, because you can use it at anytime and you don't have to worry about them hunting you down for dumping them. Just make sure that it isn't a lover that you are likely to bump into in the street. I think I may have used the working abroad story on over 10 different women in the past, and it works so well.

You just have to hope that they don't ask to come and visit you, because you can say that you will be working on the road so you won't be at a fixed place for too long. If they try to start an argument or prevent you from going you can easily say "You knew my job might require me to work away when you met me so why are you making it hard for me?"

It is usually advisable that if your lover becomes a possessive bunny boiler then it's always best to end it before it becomes dangerous to your marriage or real relationship. It is a cruel and harsh world being a cheater, but if you want to do it successfully then you need to be mean, but do not be seen as being mean. You have to be careful that you do not come home with any love bites or scratches because these are not easy to get away with. If you feel that someone is about to give you a love bite, try and pull away and say, "I do not like them, they are known to cause skin cancer." And yes that is a fact, that repetitive damage to the skin and small blood vessels under the skin can cause cancer.

So you do not have to explain yourself anymore than that. But if you do end up with a mark, then a thick jumper or foundation can cover it.

I have explained what to say to lovers when they ask you why your phone is always off, but I did not go into detail about what to say if your partner asks why your normal phone is off. After all they will know that you have signal in your area and if you are on contract then they will know you have credit, so what do you do in this situation? A lie will not always work both ways so you may need to think up a completely new story.

The faulty phone lie may work, but if your phone is on the blink and they know it, then it is a bonus. You can of course tell your partner that you forgot to take your phone with you or the battery died, but there is only so many times that these lies will work before your partner will start to get suspicious. You can instead say that you were so tired you fell asleep or weren't feeling well, or that you have had so many phone calls from people that you wanted 5 minutes peace so you turned the phone off. All these are simple excuses but they work. You only need to use them if you are asked, so do not feel the need to waste an excuse by saying, "if you tried to call me today then you wouldn't have got through because I fell asleep." You may have completely wasted a lie and when you really do need to use it, then you are stuck because you can't keep mysteriously falling asleep all the time.

When I told some of my friends that I was writing this book, they all started laughing and said, if someone was going to write it then there is nobody better than the master himself. I thought this was quite funny because they all seem to think that its funny to call me the master, because I have never been caught, but I do not see myself as a master at all, I do think that I have been very lucky, and some of that luck can be put down to my careful planning, especially as I have had a few close calls before. As I mentioned before my ex girlfriend was very jealous and possessive, if I were to look at a girl on TV then she would automatically accuse me of having an affair with her.

It could have been Pamela Anderson, I mean for god sake, when am I going to get the chance to fly out to Los Angeles and have an affair with one of the most gorgeous girls in the world? I would wait till the weekend of course. Ha Ha! Well I can honestly say that no I haven't had an affair with Pamela Anderson or anyone else of her calibre, but the thought of it had crossed my mind before. The point I am trying to make is that my ex was always suspicious of me and anyone else that came into contact with me.

I once pointed out an ex girlfriend to her in a nightclub, she then met up with her in the toilet and warned her off me, I mean how stupid is that? It wasn't even like I was talking to the ex girlfriend at all, I just spotted her and pointed her out to my current girlfriend at the time and she assumed that she would try to get back with me. Having a partner like this does not make your life very easy if you plan to cheat, but I had the bonus of not living with her, because I know my life would have been a nightmare. Not only would I not of been able to get a chance to cheat, but I wouldn't even be able to see any of my friends.

Saying that she made it very hard for me to see my friends then, but she did say to me that she was possessive over me because she loved me so much and didn't want to lose me, but its ironic that this was how she did eventually lose me because I could not handle the pressure of having to be told what to do, what to wear, who I can and can't talk to. For a while after the end of this relationship I felt free, it was unusual because I was not actually seeing anyone else when I broke up with her.

So for once I became a single person. This seemed so strange to me because I always had someone to go to, and somewhere to stay. I enjoyed being single for a few weeks, at last I had the chance to do anything I wanted. No longer did I have to keep one eye on the clock because I had to make sure I was on time to be somewhere else. I spent about 3 weeks to a month just chilling out and doing my own thing, but I eventually became bored so I wanted to find another girlfriend. As you can imagine it did not take me very long, I met most of my girlfriends from the Internet. I think about 80% of my girlfriends are Internet women. I find it so much easier to meet people without leaving your house and spending money in a bar. Sometimes I would try and see how many phone numbers I could score in a day.

I think my record is 3. You have to remember that people are more careful about giving their details out on the Internet because they want to know they can trust you first. It can sometimes take all day before you can get a number while other times it can only take a few messages, it all depends on the person you are talking to. People at my work knew what I was up to because

I would do the same thing there as well, and I got the nickname "Internet stud."

I was quite impressed with that, because I used to be very shy in my teen years, I used to be bullied at school because I was small fat with NHS glasses and braces, so it wasn't until I was about 19-23 before my confidence became what it is now. No longer am I shy or nervous, I have a very good way with people. I am always the agony uncle to my friends and I am very well known for getting information from people without asking a direct question, its all about hinting about something until you get the answer you want to hear.

I do it all the time to my friends and they still do not realise I am doing it. This can be very useful when you are cheating. Here is an example, say that your lover keeps talking about a cousin or a friend of theirs that sounds just like your partner. Instead of asking what their name is what you want to do is hint things at them and they may actually answer the question that is on your mind. What I mean by hinting is very simple is if your partner is called Sally, and your lover is telling you all about their cousin that sounds just like her then you could change the subject and say, "I used to have a pet dog called Sally. I can't remember why I called her that, because it is a name you don't hear very much anymore." That is the hint, because if your lover's cousin is actually called Sally she will say, "that's my cousin's name. So it's not that unusual" You will now be in trouble, so in this situation you will use the working abroad cover to get away before she wants to introduce you to her family. However on the other hand if she does not say anything, then the cousin just sounds like Sally and probably isn't her at all.

This is just one situation at hinting, but it is a very clever talent I have to finding out everything I want to know without asking a single question. Just remember not to be too obvious with the hint. Change the subject if you have to or you can play the innocent and make out that you don't know anything. Act like you are really interested in what they have to say just to keep them talking and get more information out of them. Hinting isn't a unique trick that can only be used when cheating you can use it in every day life even if you are trying to get the truth out of someone, by playing stupid and acting like you don't know anything, keep playing them for more information or hint at them till they tell you what you want to hear.

Now we will go into affairs at work. In these situations one or both parties may or may not be married and they are aware that the other person is married too. Office affairs are usually based on sex and adventure. The couple may try to have sex in the office or pop out during breaks to have sex, mostly because of the risk of getting caught. It can be a thrill that enhances sexual pleasure. After all what do you think the boss will say if he walks into his office and finds 2 of his employees across his desk in an intimate position?

He will not be best pleased, unless you or your lover is the boss then you can pretty much do what you want. However office romances may not be just about sex, they could be formed on the triangle points that I mentioned earlier. You both may be unhappy in your marriage, so you both confide in each other to make it better. There can be a good thing about having a lover that knows you are married or attached and that is you don't have to lie so much. They will know why your phone will be off, and they know not to call or text you at home. They will also know what you are doing when not at the office so it will save a lot of lies. But the problem of them knowing you are married can be used against you if things go wrong, so be careful of this.

I have had a few lovers that knew I had a girlfriend and it really is a comfort to know that they still want to be with you regardless. And you feel so much better knowing that you don't need to lie every five minutes, but for insurance it is better that you still give your stealth telephone number and do not talk to much about your wife/husband because this is just as good as the hinting trick I told you about earlier, except they are getting the information they want to hear from you.

It's always better to give away as little as possible about your home life, because you do not want it to be used against you in a bunny boiler situation. You must also remember that if your lover is aware that you are attached to someone else, you still must not be seen in public in the same town as your partner, because it still causes hassle if you are seen out and you have to explain that it was only your work colleague or boss.

Whether or not your lover is aware of your partner, it can be an ideal thing to take them to a hotel, for a little getaway. Just try and make sure that the hotel is booked in their name or another name. Pay with cash if possible, because hotels leave big marks on your bank statements, and this is not good, especially if your statements are being monitored. Something very simple can be overlooked when you are cheating and that is your condom supply. If you and your partner use condoms, then when you go to visit your lover make sure you have your own separate stash. This may seem trivial, but you do not know if your partner counts the condoms and if there is one or two missing, then you may have to face some answers. As mentioned before, cheating always leaves a trail of evidence, that must be covered up and that goes for your supply of condoms as well.

People can sometimes sense it when they know they have been found out, it can also be paranoia, but if you think that your partner is suspicious or knows about your affair but doesn't let on, then you still have to remain on top of the situation. It may be an idea to stop seeing your lover for a little while, tell them that you are under a bit of stress and you need to get away for a while, anything that will stop them trying to call you or meet you. It is a fact that if a partner becomes suspicious then they are 10 times more observant on the little things that usually get overlooked. Anything you say or do will be examined under a microscope, so you have to be extra careful what you do in this stage. Try not to do anything out of the ordinary and do not give them any reason to get suspicious about you. If they think that you are spending too much time at the gym or with friends than usual, then organise to go to these places but invite them with you or go on your own and call them from the place where you usually say you go.

This way they may still be suspicious but you have given them reason to believe that you are telling the truth. Try and see if your partner plans to catch you out, and if they are then you probably need to look at what you have done to arise suspicion. If they approach you and tell you about their growing suspicions, then listen carefully, because they will nearly always explain why they think you are cheating. It might be an unusual number appearing on the phone bill or too many late nights at the office, but listen carefully and play the innocent. You will be able to learn and adapt to this later on, by not coming home late every night or not using the home phone all the time. (Not that you should use the home phone to call lovers, as this is evidence.)

You have to now try and convince them that there is nothing going on, and that a relationship is based on trust, if you don't have trust then you don't have anything. If they still don't believe you then you can turn the table round and make them feel guilty, it is a cruel thing to do, but it works well. Basically threaten to walk out on them, say that you have done nothing wrong and you will not be with someone who does not trust you or thinks you are a liar. Its all about reverse psychology, they may have planned to leave you if they didn't like the sound of your explanation, but you will make them think they are in the wrong for being paranoid and you will leave them. It is something they won't see coming, but most of the time it works. This must only be used if the argument does not favour you. By now you should be very good at lying and you would hopefully have a story planned out for this situation. If all is going well and it seems like they believe your story, do not assume that you should carry on seeing your lover as normal. As a security measure, you should still lay low for a while, think how close you came to being found out in the first place. Sit down and rethink your future. Should you continue to see your lover, should you play it differently? After a while you may get sloppy in your routine and this is when accidents happen or you are found out.

People get used to the routine and become confident in what they are doing, you may think, well I haven't been found out yet so why bother making all the extra effort in covering it up? It is the extra effort you have put in that is why you haven't been found out. The same thing goes if your lover suspects that you are cheating on them, (if they do not know you are married or have a partner.) you have to try and convince them that you are not, but it may be a little harder doing it this way around, especially if they have never been around your house and you don't always have your phone on. You can still use the reverse psychology on them about the trust thing, this is effective both ways, but at the end of the day, your lover may not be worth the hassle and it may be just easier to sit back and let them finish you. After all your partner or marriage is far more important than a bit on the side so to some, it may not be worth trying to fight over, it is all down to personal opinion.

Finally, say that you have read up to this point and you think you have everything covered. You are confident that all your tracks have been concealed and you have all your alibis, but your partner senses something suspicious. What could they be suspicious about? They believe your story on where you were, and yes there is no emails or phone evidence, so what is giving it away? Your behaviour is the answer to that one.

Many people who find happiness from somewhere else become less caring and less loving to their real partner, and sometimes they do not realise it. You might not say, "I love you" as much, or do not seem to be interested in the little things that you used to. Or you may not make love as much or not at all. All these examples will arise suspicion because you are acting out of character, and without an explanation, can make things worse. You must try and make sure that you do not stray outside of your normal behaviour patterns because this will show that something is wrong. The best way to prevent this from happening is to take a big look at yourself and see if you have noticed any differences from one week to the next, and if so, sort it out before it gets noticed.

Some people find it hard to go through an interrogation and will eventually crack when it seems like the argument is not being won. If you feel that no matter what you say or do does not get any positive results, then keep it up. It does not matter if the evidence is against you all the way, you must stand your ground and fight your innocence. This may seem futile after a certain point, but if you finally give in then nothing you say after that will be believed again, even if you tell the truth in the future. As far as I am concerned you have only been caught out when you are caught in bed with someone else or if your partner leaves you. Anything else can be fixed by planning your defence and knowing what to say next. It doesn't matter if your partner approaches you and says, "My mate saw you holding hands with another person in the town." This doesn't mean you have been caught out. Firstly it's secondary evidence and can be proved wrong. It also means you haven't been as careful as you could have been, and now you have to pay for it by convincing your partner that it wasn't you. By simply taking control of the situation and saying that you were at work that day and it could have been someone who looked like you, will mean all the difference. And if your story is convincing enough, you will be given the benefit of the doubt. There is a little trick that can be very useful when you think that your defence doesn't stand up. However it only works if you have a stealth phone. What you do is put the number of your stealth phone into your normal phone, but put it in under the name of one of your closest friends. (Obviously, don't put it in as "stealth phone.") Here is the clever part, have a little text conversation between each of the phones. First what you do is text your stealth phone saying something like "Sarah doesn't trust me, she thinks I was with another woman last Tuesday." Then text back to your normal phone "That is stupid. You were with me on Tuesday night, and if you were seeing someone else you would have told me about it."

Can you see where this is going? Keep the conversation going between the phones for about 2-5 texts and stop. Then if you have a nosey partner that is prone to looking through your phone, they will see the messages in your inbox and outbox and believe that you were out with your friend on Tuesday night like you said you were. This does not always work if you show them the text messages in the middle of an argument. Most people know that friends will cover up for each other and assume that the messages are acted. That is why its better for them to find the messages themselves, because it is so much more convincing. Obviously if you have already put the messages on there before the argument, especially if your partner has made it clear he/she is suspicious of you then that is good prior planning and can be used to stop the argument, but it won't work if you try to send the text messages a few hours or days later. I call this phantom texting, because the sender isn't a real person, you are in fact texting yourself. This kind of phantom texting also works well if you want to cover yourself before you actually do something. By this I mean phantom text your normal phone, "Hi mate, would you like to come over tomorrow night, I am feeling down and need company." Then obviously tell your partner that you got a text and you need to see your friend. Keep it convincing by phantom texting the time when you will meet and what you plan to do when you get there. Sometimes your partner may want to come with you, especially if they are friendly with the person you are pretending to meet, but just make out that they are having woman problems or something and its better that you go alone.

You may think it is a waste of time doing this before you actually go out, but there is a reason for it. Obviously your partner isn't going to be suspicious if you say you have made plans to see your friend, but if for whatever reason something happens that may question your whereabouts, then you have it covered. The thing about text messages is that they are all logged with who sent the message and at what time they were sent. If your partner seems suspicious about where you were then show them the text messages. They will then see your staged text conversations arranging to meet were sent a day or two ago and you were where you said you would be. They may not be convinced by the text messages and might try to call the number. But because it's the number of your stealth phone and should be switched off. They will only get the answer machine, which may buy you some time. If this happens you need to contact your friend and let them know that they may get asked if you were with them the other night. Just make sure it is a friend that is willing to help cover for you and you tell them everything they need to know just in case the suspicious Sarah tries to catch them out.

This phantom texting can also work the same way with emails, the only difference is you have to make a phantom email address.

Alternatively you can also use the name of the person who you are suspected to be having an affair with. Make a phantom email address or put their name into your phonebook. And do the same thing, as before the only difference is that the email or texts would go something like this, "Sarah seems to think that I am cheating on her with you." The return message will be something like, "That's crazy, surely she should know I am seeing someone else and I don't think of you in that way." These set ups are very effective, because like I said before, if Sarah checks up on the phone or computer she will see the conversation and realise that there is nothing going on. If there was something going on and you were emailing a real person, then the messages would naturally say something like

"Sarah knows about us."

"Oh no we better end it now."

So your phantom conversations will completely throw her off track and make her rethink their suspicions and stop worrying. It is simple but very effective.

I am going to mention again about deleting your emails and text messages, for the simple reason that I once nearly got caught out because I didn't listen to my own advice and became sloppy. I kicked myself for not being careful but luckily enough I was able to talk my way out of it. Using Msn messenger has the same problem as email because many people use this tool to communicate with others and it stores all your contacts. The last thing you need is your partner logging in to your account and asking who they all are. Msn also has a conversation-logging tool enabled for parents to keep tabs on who their children are talking to, for obvious reasons and that is to prevent paedophiles from luring children out. Your partner could be storing all your private conversations and checking up on you without you knowing, so if you do use Msn to chat to your lover, always make sure that you haven't got the "save conversations" option enabled. A safer way to use Msn is to use the net version, because this has limited functions and will not log any of your conversations, which is a good thing.

Or you could make up a completely new Msn profile that you will keep secret from your partner. This is a good idea, because you can then have your clean profile and also have your secret profile. If you use dating or friends websites, then make sure that you keep your password secret and change it from time to time, to ensure that you won't be hacked. If your partner discovers your Msn or Outlook password, then they effectively have control over all your other sites you use. Because it is so easy to get hold of some ones Internet passwords if you have access to their email account. What I mean is, if your partner looks through the computer history (hopefully they should not have done if you cleared it.) and finds that you have registered with a dating site, then they may try to log in. If they don't know your password, then most websites that rely on usernames and password access usually have a tab saying "forgotten your password?" if your partner clicks on this then the website will send the password to your email address. If your partner has access to your email account then they will get the email with the password and then will be able to access all your profiles and see who you have been talking to.

PART FOUR

TRUE STORIES

In this section I will tell you about some of my experiences and some of the times when I have come close to being caught. I will keep the identity of all the people involved secret as I respect peoples right to privacy. Not to mention I still see to some of my ex girlfriends and would hate for them to read this and find out that I am talking about them. The first story involves the closest I ever came to getting caught, and it put me to the test on how well I had planned my cover story. I was with my possessive girlfriend, and I had another girlfriend that lived a few miles away in a town called Hemel Hempstead. I went with one of my friends to see her and we set up a little double date. We were all hanging out in a field with the car. One day when I was laying by a tree with my lover, my friend's new girlfriend was sitting in the car with him. She played around with his phone on the games and must have looked up my number.

The problem was that my friend only had my real number stored on his phone and not my stealth number, so she added my real number to her phone.

I think you can see how this was a problem, because now they had both my real and stealth numbers and I didn't even know. I took my new girlfriend to a hotel one night and we had a good time. However 2 weeks later when I was sitting with my real partner, I got a text out of the blue asking me to call my lover. My partner saw the text and called the number on the display. To make things worse she even put it on loudspeaker. I was now facing both my girlfriend and my lover at the same time, and I honestly thought my time was up. My lover was telling my girlfriend how I had been seeing her and I slept with her in a hotel, not to mention she gave an excellent description of me and the clothes I wore. I was standing there saying, that I did not know who she was even though she was on the phone saying I did know her.

Eventually the conversation had ended and my partner was very upset, but I remained cool. I told her to phone the hotel and ask if there had been a reservation in my name. So she phoned up the hotel that I was "supposed" to have stayed at and they checked their records and they told her they did not have any records of a Mr D Jones ever staying at their hotel. (Remember how I said do not sign into hotels with your real name?)

She was convinced that I had not spent a night in a hotel with this girl, but she still needed answers on how she knew so much about me and had my number. I convinced her that it was an Internet stalker who had started messaging me on an Internet friends website. I explained how my profile had many details about myself including photos of me wearing the clothes that she had described on the phone. I said that she was a girl who started talking to me but would not take no for an answer because she knew I had a girlfriend. I then explained that my hotmail account had been hacked into and she had taken my number down from my registration details. I told my girlfriend that the Internet stalker knew I would be with you, so she deliberately sent a text to get you suspicious and leave me so she could finally have me for herself. In my girlfriends mind this started to make sense and she believed the story I told her. I also had an advantage, because everyone knew that I was very good with computers so I knew that it is possible to get information about anyone on the planet if you know what you are doing.

This made me realise how close I came, but I never spoke to my secret girlfriend again, because her impatience in asking me to call her nearly cost me everything.

It makes me laugh when I watch programmes like Eastenders or friends, because they always have a storyline where someone is having an affair, and the truth always comes out in the end. They never have a story where someone gets away with being unfaithful. The writers like to make sure that the naughty cheating character always gets caught eventually so they try and educate the viewers that cheating won't work. Well, unfortunately real life isn't Eastenders, and in most cases on TV shows, the ways in which the actor is found out is so pathetic and unrealistic. Here is an example, say that Den Watt's had a mistress, the show would have him walking through Albert square with her in broad daylight in public, holding hands. This is so unlikely because Den lives in the square, his wife lives in the square and everybody who knows him lives in the square. And it will always be one of the neighbours that spot him kissing her outside the Queen Victoria pub or something similar. Nobody in their right mind would do something this risky in their own street, but it is always how they play the story.

Back to reality, now and another true story, on how I dealt with a situation that could have been taken the wrong way. I had a secret lover that was aware that I had a girlfriend. She also lived a few towns away from me, so I was relatively safe from being seen in public. We were walking down the street in her town and one of my partners friends bumped into me when I was with her. She saw me first and said hello. I turned around, smiled and said hello back. I introduced my lover as my cousin. I explained that she was on a break from university in Leeds and my uncle had told me to show her around. I even said to the friend that we were going for coffee and would she be interested in joining us. Luckily she had other plans, but it was a close call, and would not have worked if my lover did not know I was attached to someone else.

If there is anything I have learnt in the past on how to get away with something and that is to be blatant. If I had told my girlfriend's friend that the person I was with was just a friend then, it could have gone a completely different way. But by saying that she was my cousin and even having the front to ask the friend if she wanted to join us for a coffee, made it so clear that there was nothing to worry about. However if your partner knows that you do not have a cousin or family member that you can pass off as, then you may need to think of someone that will eliminate being a possible lover. You could say it's your secretary or an old school friend that you haven't seen for years, you just have to be blatant with your story. Usually this will not get back to your partner and if it does then the chances are that they won't mention it to you and will think nothing of it. Everything will be fine so long as you do not act like you have been caught out.

With all the above advice you should now have a better and safer way of how to cheat. Hopefully if you stick to the guide nothing should go wrong. Things do have a habit of going wrong, as you well know, so you have to know what to expect when you get found out and dumped. I have only come close to being caught in the past and I have to say, the emotions you go through afterwards are not very comforting at all. You will feel low, guilty, upset and will regret everything. You will tell yourself that you won't do it again. When you have a lot to lose like a house and a family, I cannot explain how you would feel if you lost it all. But you will be kicking yourself for being so foolish, all you want is to turn back the clock and fix the problem before it went wrong. You won't be able to do that, but instead you will have to prepare yourself for an emotional ride for a couple of weeks maybe even months before you can get over it. Just ask yourself before you do anything with someone else, "is this worth it? Can I handle this and get away with it?" You will not know the answer to that, but at least if you are prepared for it, then you can see for yourself.

Section Two:
Is My Partner
Cheating?

In this section I will turn the tables around and explain what to do if your partner is cheating on you and how to find out. Now as unusual as this may sound, but I have been cheated on in the past and it is not a nice thing to have happen. You will feel betrayed, heartbroken and very, very hurt. Sometimes you won't see it coming, or things may happen that cause you to get suspicious. However, you must not automatically assume that your partner is cheating on you without proof. Hunches and secondary evidence isn't any good.

It will not stand up very well if you confront your partner because they can easily talk their way out of it. You have to make sure that you have as much evidence as possible to make it impossible for them to deny it. So firstly you must not question them or make them aware that you are suspicious, because if they think you are on their back, then they will make it harder for you to prove anything. You have to try and keep your emotions at bay and remain strong-minded. I do hope that there is nothing to worry about, paranoia can be a very dangerous thing and it has a habit of clouding your judgement and making you jump to conclusions. I can be very paranoid a lot of the time and it really does not help. I can prove that you can never be 100% sure that your partner won't cheat on you, because It happened to me with the person I very least suspected it.

The ex that I talk about in this book, the one that was very paranoid and jealous, cheated on me. It took me 3 years after splitting up with her before she actually told me. She despised cheating, said they needed to be hung, she really put her point across clear and simple that she did not like it. However, it turns out that on a drunken night out she cheated on me with one of her friends when I was at work. Now to me this opened my eyes a bit, because she was the last person on Earth I would have expected to cheat, because she protested against it throughout the 2 years we were together and yet she did it herself. We are both to this day very good friends and always talk about the old times, but it took us 3 years before we both finally let the truth out Now if you have bought this book for the sole reason to find out if you have been cheated on, then you really should still read the first section on how to be a successful cheat. You will be able to find out a cheater so much easier if you know how they operate.

PART FIVE

SPOTTING THE SIGNS

No relationship is trouble free, it doesn't matter who you are or how much money you have. Men and women argue all the time and there are always problems that come up in life to test your strength as a couple. I think that people do not put enough effort into a relationship or a marriage as much as they used to in the old days. That is why divorce has a high statistic and people are always breaking up. I have heard that a couple split up over something as stupid as an argument over who was watching what on the TV.

Life is too short to worry about the trivial things, and love and trust are both very hard to earn, and when you lose it then it is hard to get back. I am a very laid back person and I never let things get to me, but I have been with women that have pushed my patience to the limit and most of the time it has been over trivial things. No disrespect meant here, but women get emotional very easily and take things to heart, they complain more than men. They get paranoid easier and worry more. If you tell another man something he will know what you are talking about. But sometimes if you tell a woman the same thing, she can take it the wrong way and you have to explain it differently for her to understand.

This can happen with men as well, some men can have female emotions and temperaments that have the same effect. You have to understand your partner and how they deal with their emotions. I have a natural ability to read people when I get to know them. I know what they are capable of, what they are likely to do in any situation and what they are thinking. This can come as an advantage because building up a profile on someone lets me know what is going on in their head and what they are likely to do next.

The most obvious signs that your partner is cheating are listed below. If you recognise one or all of the signs, do not automatically assume that they must be cheating, because they might not be, the fact is you have to observe these signs and investigate where necessary.

1. Partner may lack or stop giving you attention
2. Partner is no longer interested in sex or sex becomes a rare occurrence.
3. Partner spends more time than usual at work or out elsewhere.
4. Partner suddenly becomes hard to get hold of and nobody knows where they are.
5. You may find that some of the stories they tell of where they have been do not seem logical, or the story changes when told at another time.
6. Partner tells lies, or you find out by other people that your partner was not where they said they were.
7. A lot of unusual numbers keep appearing on the phone bill or there are unusual purchases on bank statements. (Hotels, Jewellers, etc...)

8. Partner smells of aftershave/perfume when they shouldn't
9. Condom supplies have decreased more than normal
10. A friend tells you that they saw your partner with another person
11. You can sense something is wrong due to their attitude or behaviour pattern
12. You are suspicious that your partner seems to spend a lot of time with a work colleague or friend of the opposite sex
13. Your partner has suspicious emails or text messages on their phone and pc

As you can see from this list there are more signs on finding out a cheater than being found out by a partner. There are many more but there is no point in listing all of them, because with this guide you will pretty much find out everything out need to know.

If you are reading this section specifically then there must be a reason for it. You must feel that your partner is up to something and you want to know what it is, so why do you think your partner is cheating on you? Why would they do it? I have given a few scenarios in section one that explains what drives people to cheat, but there can be many more reasons. Do you have an idea why they would betray you, or seek the attention from another person? There can be many little hints or clues left by the person, you just have to notice them.

They might have said that the sex isn't fulfilling, or they may get frustrated that they want to try something sexual, but you won't do it because you think it sounds horrible. It might be a case that you are having to many arguments, or you both are not happy with each other. Another one could be that they are dependant on your love and security but you don't give them enough to satisfy their needs. And finally there may be no signs at all. In this case you may need to do even more investigating because if there are no obvious signs that they are cheating, then the truth is, they probably are not.

The first thing you have to do is write down all your suspicions, what may have caused them to cheat, when you think they are meeting the other person and finally if you have an idea, who the other person might be. With all these in mind you have the base to start your investigation. The only other thing you need is courage, confidence and be very cunning.

PART SIX

INVESTIGATION

Now you are all ready to do the investigating, you have to know where to start. The best place is the root of what caused your suspicions. I am going to start with suspicious phone numbers on the phone bill. Now if you find that there are a lot of unknown numbers appearing on the bill, go through your phone and see if they match any in your phone book. If it is a landline, check the area code and see if you can find which town it comes from. If you do not know which town it comes from, then look up area codes on the Internet via search engine. If you get a chance, look through your partners phone and see if the number comes up in his phone book. It could simply be one of their friends that you don't have the number to. And finally, call the number, see who answers the phone. Simply say that their number has appeared on your phone bill and you were just curious who it was. If they ask you who you are then tell them the truth, say that you are Joe Bloggs, married to Jane Bloggs. See if this causes a reaction. Something like "She told me she was single"

However if the person does not give you an answer or has no idea why their number is listed on your phone bill, just say, "I am sorry I must have you mixed up with someone else." Put the phone down, but do not think that this is the end to the investigation. If you did not get a reaction or they did not give you the answers you need, then you go to plan B. Ask your partner if they recognise the number. Do not tell them that you have phoned them up, just play innocent and ask. After all, you are perfectly in your own right to question unknown numbers.

If your partner says that they do not recognise the number, then say, "Ok, well I better phone it up and see who it is." If you say that, then they might try and stop you and suddenly remember that it is a "friend's" number or something like that. Then ask which friend, hopefully you have taken the name of the person when you called them earlier and see if the names match. If the person on the phone said their name was Jim, and your partner says that the number belongs to a friend called Mary, then obviously your partner is lying. The reason why it is your partner lying and not the person on the phone is because if anyone answers the phone to somebody they don't know and the caller asks who you are, then you have no reason to lie and will tell them just to find out who they are and what they want.

You are now faced with a decision, you could confront them and say "That's funny, because I called the number earlier and the person who answered wasn't called Mary, It was a man named Jim." If you chose to do this, without any other proof, then you might lose the battle if your partner is quick and clever enough to talk their way out of it and say, "Yes that's Jim's wife." I would advise against confronting them yet as you can still gather up more of a case against them. The other alternative if you are sure that the person on the phone is having an affair with your partner, is to confront your partner and pretend you know everything, say something long the lines of "I was on the phone to your friend Mary earlier and she told me everything, about your affair and that you have been cheating on me." 9 times out of 10 they will say that she is lying, but you never know they may confess everything, or fall apart under the strain. However using this approach may not always work very well if you are not 100% sure that the person on the phone is having an affair with your partner. Like I said before, you must not let paranoia get in the way. But if you decide to use the first approach then swallow your pride, fight against the urge to question them any further and leave it at that.

What you do in the meantime is look deeper into the call. Wait until the next phone bill comes in and see if the number comes up again. If it does then look at the times when the calls were made, were you at home? If all the calls were made when you were out then obviously something must be going on. If the calls were made from the house phone then there is something you can do to find out what is going on. Look at the times of the calls and see if there is a pattern. Are the calls only made on a Wednesday evening when you are out shopping, if so, then its time to do a bit of James Bond surveillance. If you have a home video camera or a tape recorder, then you are in luck. Set either or both up by the phone and make sure they are well hidden. Start recording the second you leave the house and make sure you are not seen doing this. When you come back and your partner is out of the way, then play back the video/audio tape and see if you picked up anything.

If you did then listen carefully to the conversation, see if it sounds suspicious, and check your bill to see if it was the same number called. Hopefully if you have picked up anything, and it is without a doubt, a call to another lover, then you will have enough evidence to confront your partner, and now could also be the best time to adopt the second option of making out you know everything from the person on the phone. In this situation, there is little they can say in their defence, especially if you prove that they lied about who the number belonged to. However this plan may not always work for a number of reasons, they may not call the person at the time when you set up the recording, the tapes may run out before anything happens, or if it's a cordless phone, then your partner may walk out of the room and talk somewhere else in the house. All I can say is don't give up, if you didn't get a result the first time, keep at it, you may eventually catch something. There is another way around this problem and that is to get your phone tapped. Yes you read right, bugging your phone like you see in films with spies, anybody can do it. The only problem is that it is illegal. By law it is considered to be invasion of privacy and breaches the data protection act. The only time the police are allowed to do it is if they have a warrant authorized by a judge. Saying that, it's illegal to use a phone tap, but it's not illegal to buy and own one. Pointless really but that's the way the law works. You can get all kinds of spy surveillance equipment from mini cameras, to phone bugs.

You just have to know where to look.

Do a search on Ebay or Google. Search for "Spy equipment." You will get an unlimited amount of responses. The more high tech equipment may be a little bit expensive but you are always sure to find something that will do the trick. The clever thing about phone taps is that they are only activated when the phone connects to a line, so you do not need to worry what time and where the phone is used. It will all be recorded and saved to a receiver that you will be able to playback whenever you want. You won't be able to do this with mobile phones, and also if your partner is using his/her mobile to call the number then it is even harder for you to try and catch them out with the camcorder or audio recorder. The plus side to this is that if your partner is using their mobile phone, then there is more chance of finding evidence on the phone, from text messages. Saying that you still might be able to catch them out on their mobile if they are using it in the house when you have the recording equipment set up. Another bonus if you can get hold of it is to check the mobile phone bill as well. You will see if the number shows up, you might even find a few more unknown numbers come to that. You will also see how many text messages were sent to the number as well depending on the sort of phone your partner uses.

If the phone calls persist and you have recorded evidence, you can try a different approach. Call the number and say "Hello I called you a little while ago and asked who you were. I now know that you are having an affair with my wife/husband, I even have recorded your phone conversations." See if you get a response from them, if you do its always better to have it recorded when they confess, because this will tighten the noose even more on your cheating partner when you produce the evidence. After all you have the phone bills with all the times the number was called, you have them on tape (hopefully a conversation you produce will be good evidence.) and finally show them your recorded phone conversation with the person admitting that your partner is in fact having an affair with them. I tell you now, not even Michael Jackson's lawyers will be able to get your cheating partner off the hook with this evidence.

I think I have covered the phone surveillance as best as I can now, but let's have a look at computer surveillance. I am a very talented person with a computer, I know them inside out and anybody who knows me will back me up when I say that I am a "computer whiz kid." With this in mind, if anybody thought that they could do anything on my computer without me knowing then, they are sorely mistaken. That has been put into practice, because I had suspicions about my ex and my pc was rigged up so much that she couldn't even sneeze without me finding out. I can find out every move she made, gained access to her email accounts and any password she use for Internet websites such as hotmail, Msn messenger and dating sites.

Having a reasonable knowledge of the Internet can be a huge benefit, if you know what you are doing, you can have unlimited access to other peoples private lives. Get their phone numbers, addresses, bank details everything. A lot of people do not realise that the

Internet has a very dark side to it and in the wrong hands, can prove dangerous.

I remember a few years ago, Bill Gates said that he has such a powerful firewall on his computer that it would take a million years to crack it. And guess what? A 17 year old school boy managed to hack it, get hold of his bank details and used Bill Gates credit card to buy Viagra and sent it to Bill's home address. This was all over the news and when arrested the boy said "I didn't mean any harm all I did was try to prove that nobodies personal details are safe, no matter how well protected you think you are." I think Bill actually hired the boy to help out Microsoft produce software that hackers cannot beat. So this goes to show that the leader of Microsoft himself isn't safe. I am not going to explain how to get bank details or anything that can be considered illegal and I will not be held responsible for anyone who abuses the information in this guide. Firstly where would you look for clues or evidence of an affair?

I would start with Outlook Express. If you have complete access to your partners Outlook account, then check all the messages in the inbox. There could be an email from your partner's lover. This might be unlikely in some cases, because if your partner knows you have access to their emails, then they won't be careless enough to leave incriminating evidence for you to find. The next place you look is the outbox or sent messages folder. A lot of people forget that sent messages are saved in the sent or outbox folder and thus do not delete them, as well as the deleted folder. This is the most likely place that you might find something, because people put unwanted emails in the deleted folder and forget about them. It then has to be deleted again for it to be permanently removed from the computer.

Your computer may do this automatically for you so you have to make sure you keep track of all the folders on a regular basis. Did you find an email that looks out of place? If so then copy and paste it onto Microsoft word. Do this with any suspicious emails you find and save the word document in a folder that is well hidden in your computer's program files so your partner will not find it. The reason why I say copy and paste the messages to word is because they can be deleted at anytime and you will lose the evidence you have. That's not to say you can't print the emails out either which is probably a better thing to do. It may also be worth your while looking at the contacts list and see if there is anyone that should not be there. Your partner might not have anything suspicious in their messages folders, but that could be because they are very careful to delete them, or maybe they don't have anything to hide at all. It only takes one slip up to forget once to delete an email and it could be the time when you find it.

Right say for instance you try to get into Outlook Express and it is password protected, what do you do now? There is more than one way to skin a cat so do not give up yet.

Have a couple of attempts at guessing what the password is, I know this sounds impossible, but I have been lucky and guessed right in the past. The first possible password that people are keen on using are the names of their partners. Try to put your full name without spaces and see if this works. If not try typing in your first name or your surname on their own. Some passwords can be case sensitive so try it with capitals. If this doesn't work then it could be the name of your pet.

If you can't guess it then do not keep on trying because you could go on forever and still not figure it out.

Here is another way of getting the password, and that is to ask your partner what it is. Yes you heard me right, but don't ask just for the sake of it, because they won't see any reason why they should. This is what you do, make sure that your partner is out of the house and say that you need to send an important email to someone but you can't get into Outlook. Ask for the password and with a good reason like that, you should have no problem getting it. One that always works is if you phone up your partner and say that you are trying to order something from the Internet but it keeps asking for an email address. Say you don't have an email address or that your email is down. Now ask if you can use their email address instead, which will then give you a reason to have their password.

This only works if you are living with someone and share a computer with them, you cannot gain access to their Outlook account from a different computer.

A lot of people do not always use Outlook, there is another email provider called Hotmail. It is the same sort of thing as Outlook but an Internet website. You still have the same features such as inbox, outbox, deleted and sent. Hotmail also comes with a program called Msn Messenger, which I mentioned a bit earlier in section 1. It is linked to hotmail, and enables you to send and receive messages in real time over the Internet, sort of like a chat room. With msn you are able to talk to someone with a microphone or web camera. Hotmail is used by millions of people and some prefer this than Outlook. To get the password for a hotmail account just do the same thing that I mentioned earlier about asking what the password is. When you get it you now have control over so much more than just hotmail, you have access to all the other websites that your partner uses. Say for instance your partner uses websites like www. Faceparty.com which is a site for people to make new friends and possibly a new love. With face party you basically make a profile with all your details that explain a bit about yourself with a photo and other people can send messages to you. If you know your partner uses websites such as this, then try and type in the same password that you have been given for their hotmail account. Most of the time it will be the same, because people tend to use the same password for every site they use, as this is easier to remember than having more than one. The next paragraph explains about getting hold of passwords that your partner uses on websites and was explained previously in section 1 so if you have read section 1 then you may want to skip this bit.

However if the password is different, then most of the time a website will ask you if you have forgotten it. All you have to do is say you have forgotten your password, and guess what, they will send the password to your hotmail account. So as you can see if you have control over your partners hotmail account, then you will get the email.

If you do not receive the reminder email, then your partner may have more than one hotmail account, but this is unlikely. Just check Outlook Express and see if the email gets sent here instead. You now have the chance to really check up on your partner and see who they are talking to on the net. Unlike Outlook the clever thing is with Internet based sites, you don't even have to be using the same computer that your partner uses. You can check up on them at any time from any computer and they will not have a clue that you are doing it. Do the same thing as you would with Outlook and check all the folders and contacts.

Msn messenger uses the same password as hotmail so you will be able to log in without problems here. You can now set a trap with messenger because it has a parental control tool in the options menu. This is for parents to monitor their children so they can see who they are talking to on the net. You can use this feature to see who your partner is talking to, because any conversation made will be saved as a document on the computer. To activate this feature you have bring up the Msn messenger box and click on tools, then options. Then click on the "messages" tab and you should have a section that says, "message history." What you need to do is click on the box that says, "Automatically keep a history of all my conversations." There should be another box that says "save my conversations in this folder." Finally the last thing you want to do is click on "change."

Make sure that when you choose the folder for the logged messages to be saved to, that they are in a hidden folder, your partner is not likely to find. Check up on them from time to time and see if there have been any conversations that look suspicious. Unfortunately, because Msn is not a website, you will only be able to see the logged conversations if you use the same computer as your partner. Is your partner a bit of a flirt on the Internet? If they use face party or other similar sites, do they have a lot of messages in their inbox and seem to be making out that they are single? You can now try and trap them another way. Make a fake profile on the site that they are using, even put a fake photograph of someone else on your profile and make yourself sound really nice. Then send a message to your partners account and see if they write back to you. Keep the conversation going for as long as you can and see if they plan to meet or give you their phone number. If they do try to meet you, then agree. You won't be able to text or call them, because your number will show up on their phone as being their partner. They may ask if they can have your number, but just say that you are waiting to get a new mobile phone because your last one was stolen. Only call them if you are confident you can put on a fake voice and you have blocked your number when calling don't send a message saying "You cheating sod, this is your girlfriend I was testing you to see if I could trust you."

Because they will just turn around and say that they weren't really going to meet you, they were only having a bit of fun. Just imagine the look on their face when you agree to meet somewhere and you turn up instead of the person they thought they were talking to. They won't be able to give a logical explanation on why they wanted to meet someone else other than to start an affair. Especially if they have been telling you online that they are single and are really looking forward to having a new girlfriend. When they realise that they have been saying all this to their real girlfriend, there is nothing they can do to defend themselves. The only problem you have to be aware of is if they give you their number.

The other thing to check on is the computers history, not many people delete this and it is stored on your computer for 20 days. It will display every website visited and each page viewed. Sometimes this can dig up some useful information just click on the clock icon at the top of your Explore browser and it will open up the history on the left hand side of the page.

By now you should have the computer rigged up so well that they won't be able to do anything without you knowing about it, unless they are very careful.

You go through the bank statements and you find some unusual purchases made that look quite suspicious, like a hotel bill, restaurant or jewellers, how would you investigate this?

Firstly if it's a hotel bill, does your partner work for a company that requires them to stay in a hotel? Where did they say they were on the night when the hotel bill shows up on the statement? If you can remember them saying that they were doing something else than staying in a hotel, you can start to do some investigating. First you have to find out where the hotel is and the telephone number. Phone up the hotel and ask if there was a reservation for your partner the night when your bank statement says they stayed and see what they say. If they say that your partner did stay, ask if they were alone or what room they ordered. If the room is a double instead of single then you have a cause for concern. There could be a perfectly innocent explanation for why they stayed at a hotel that night, but I would still question them about it.

If you see something on the bank statement like a present bought from somewhere but if it wasn't for you, then who was it for? First off, do you have a birthday coming up? Is it close to Christmas or Valentines Day? If not and you still haven't received any gifts, then the only thing you can do is ask. You probably won't get the answer you are looking for, but why else would there be a bank statement from a florist, jewellers or something similar if you haven't been given anything? In these situations it is hard to prove anything and it can be easily talked out of. Like with the phone bill you are perfectly within your right to ask, and if you don't like the answers you are getting, then walk out. If you walk out, it may cause them to confess.

If you want to get more evidence against them, you have to hold it in for a bit longer.

Has one of your friends told you that they saw your partner out with someone else, holding hands or anything that could seem suspicious? Well first off, do not take what you have been told for granted, because your friend could have been mistaken and saw someone who looked like your partner. And when questioned, your partner will use this in their defence. You have to find out where it was, when it was and what the other person looked like. Then ask your partner where they were at the time.

Do not ask as if you are checking up on them, make it sound like you were trying to call them or something and you couldn't get through. See what they say, if it was during their work hours, it could have been a work colleague they were seen with and perfectly innocent.

If you check with their work and they say that your partner was not in that day or left early then this will give you a bit more evidence. If the time in question happened on their day off same as before, tell them that you were trying to get hold of them but you could not get in contact. If they tell you that they were with their friend Paul or someone, leave it at that for the moment. When your partner is out, phone up Paul and verify it with him, if he says yes then this could mean one of two things. Your partner was in fact with Paul that day, or Paul is covering up for your partner. Friends will do their best to help each other out, so you may not get what you need to know with this, and Paul may even warn your partner that you have been snooping. On the other hand if Paul says that he didn't see your partner on the day, then there is defiantly something going on.

If your partner seems to be spending a lot of time out with their friends or is constantly late home from work, then you will have to investigate a bit further. If you have the money then you can hire a private detective. They can be found easily on the Internet and yellow pages. However I do warn you, I am a fully qualified private detective and I know they do not come cheap. Their fees can vary and you will end up paying out for a number of different things. First, obviously for them to take up the case, and secondly they could charge you for expenses, such as petrol, hotel expenses, food and camera film. If you want to hire a private detective you have to be sure that you can afford it, and is it worth the money if nothing suspicious is uncovered? I can tell you now, any private investigator worth his salt will find something, if there is in fact anything going on. You are their client and they will want as much information on your partner as possible, like all his personal details, what car he/she drives, what they like to eat, everything.

With all this information they are able to build up a personal profile on the target and will be able to follow them everywhere they go. Maybe you cannot afford a private investigator or are not keen on a stranger knowing about your private life, so how do you fancy doing it yourself? If you have the time and patience, then you can do just as well on your own. I am now going to give you as much advice as possible on doing private investigating, as I am trained in this field so all the advice given now, is used by real detectives. First off, can you call your partner at work? If so, then phone them a couple of hours before they are due to finish and just have a general chat. Now what you need to do is take a camera or video camera and go to their work. If you have a car then perfect Just wait outside and make sure that you or your car isn't seen. Now comes the boring bit, wait and see what happens. This can go two ways, your partner will come out on time and leave. If they do, then follow them, make sure that you keep your distance and try to get another car in front of you so they won't see you in the mirror. You just have to make sure that you do not lose them. If they walk out then you will have to follow on foot. You will still have to keep your distance and make sure you are covering your face with a scarf, dark glasses or a hat. The last thing you need is for them to turn around and see you behind them. If they go into a shop or stop for whatever reason, then stop where you are and wait for them to carry on. Whether they drive to a destination or walk, you have to make sure that you stay behind them. Pull up by the pavement about 50 yards behind and wait. If they have arrived at some ones house, try and see if you are in a clear enough position to see who answers the door. If you get a clear view of the person then take a photograph or get them on video.

Try and read the body language, do they look like they are having an affair, do they kiss or hug on the doorstep? When your partner goes in, you have to assess the area. Is the street open? Are there many people about? Do you have a clear path to any of the windows? If it looks too dangerous to sneak up on the house because of the chance of being seen, then don't. If you are confident that you can get close to the house without being seen then, walk up to the window from the side if possible. Look through the window, showing as little of yourself as possible and see if you can make anything out. This is dependant on which room the window looks in.

If it is the living room, can you see them and what they are doing? Try and get this on film, if you are using a flash camera turn it off, because they will see it and turn around.

Go back to your car and wait for your partner to come out. While you are waiting you could try calling your partner and ask them what they want for dinner or how long they think they are going to be. By doing this, you can see if they are still making out that they are at work. Put the phone down and wait for them to come out. If you are likely to catch anything, now is the time, because if they are having an affair and they say goodbye on the doorstep, then this is when they will hug and kiss. Get it on film if you can. You are now faced with another choice, do you A: Quickly drive home and have it out with your partner? Or B: Get out of the car and confront your partner while he/she is walking to their car? I would pick the second option, because you have caught them red handed and there is nothing they can do to defend themselves.

Lets take a step back for a moment and begin this scene again. This time, you are waiting for your partner outside their work and they do not come out like everyone else.

Is there a back door, or another exit they could of used? You have to be sure that you know which way they come out so you know if they have in fact left the building. In some cases you may have to pick your partner up from work anyway, so you will know where they come out If there is no sign of them, wait around for a bit. I would say give it half an hour, as a minimum. Try calling them like before and ask what they want for dinner, listen carefully for any background noises or other people in the room. I would not advise getting out of your car for a closer look, because if its an office building, there may be CCTV and people are more likely to report you to the police or on site security if you are snooping around. All you can really do here is wait. If your partner is staying behind late from work and all the employees leave on time, then hopefully your partner should finally leave the office on their own. If they come out with someone from the opposite sex, then do not jump the gun just yet or get out the car for that matter.

Like I have said it could be completely innocent. When you are at home with your partner eating dinner or watching TV etc… Ask them if they are on their own when they stay behind. If they ask why, then just say because you don't want them to be the only one in the office who has to be late home. If you get told that they are the only person who stays behind, then obviously you know it's a lie. Repeat the surveillance and see if it is the same person who leaves with your partner or see if they come out on their own. If on occasion your partner does leave the building on their own, then it probably is just a case that they have to work late and your paranoia has got the better of you. However, like the first scenario, if they leave with the same person every time, keep an eye out for that body language I told you about. Do they hug or kiss before getting into their cars? I do hope you remembered your camera.

Everybody works in different industries, so it may not be as simple as just waiting outside an office block, especially if your partner works on a building site, McDonalds or even a restaurant. You have to try and find a way that is best for waiting outside where you won't be seen, but alternatively giving you a clear view of what is going on. Your partner might not even drive to a house, it could be high-rise flats, which will not give you a chance to get a closer look. Or your partner might just drive home, and in this case you have to think of an explanation on why you have just pulled up outside your own house when you should be inside waiting for them. Usually a shopping bag full of food will get you out of this one. I have to say that if you are doing surveillance on someone, it doesn't always go as easily as I have described here. You have to be 100% sure that something is going on before you follow people around, because you may find that there is in fact nothing going on at all.

The same thing goes for when you follow your partner when they aren't working. If you live with your partner it is very hard to follow them if you have to walk out the door the same time as them, but fortunately if you do not live with your partner you can get around this problem far easier because you can be waiting outside about 50 feet away from the house. The only problem is you could be waiting outside the house all day and nothing happens. On a bad day, they won't leave the house or will not have any visitors, and if you do not have much patience, then you will not last long doing this. It usually helps if they have already told you that they can't see you from 10am onwards because they are out, then you know to get to their house at 9am and see where they go. Remember the importance of covering your face and not wearing clothes that your partner has seen you wear before. If they go to a pub for a drink, then if you are confident that you won't be recognised, go into the pub and sit as far away from your partner as possible, but within clear sight of them. Wait for them to go to the bar first, because the last thing you need is to end up standing side by side waiting to get served. If your partner meets up with friends in the pub, then they could be telling the truth. If they are in there on their own, they might be waiting for someone.

Stick around and see what happens, if someone does come in to meet your partner make sure you keep a close eye on what is going on, and do nothing, until you have visual proof of an affair. When following someone you are at risk of being seen all the time so it can be better if you do it with a friend, it's a bonus if you take a friend that your partner has not met before because they have the chance of getting much closer than you can.

I wouldn't recommend sending any of your friends out on their own to do surveillance, because friends are not always helpful and you can never be 100% sure with the results. After all they may not know your partner as well as you, so if they say "I saw him going into a house with another woman." They are not going to know who the woman is especially if it is a cousin or his sister. You are likely to know their friends and work colleagues better so it's up to you to do the surveillance and tick off people who are unlikely to be the secret lovers. Not to mention your friends may only have your best interests at heart and may try and exaggerate the story so it really is better if you get to see it first hand. Now say for instance you do not have time or it is not possible to follow your partner about or sit outside their work, there is an alternative. Remember at the start of this section when I mentioned about the mysterious phone numbers?

Call them up and find out who they are, just as I mentioned. If you are completely sure that this person is the one who is having an affair with your partner, you can find out where they live quite easily. Make sure you get hold of their full name and hopefully the town they live in (Don't ask for their town, hopefully the area code in the number should give it away.) Then you can find out where they live by the electoral poll register. Call up the local office, found in the yellow pages and ask for the address of the person on the poll and if you are asked why you need the details, be creative. Say you are a family member who has lost contact with the person, or that you are a new employer and need to verify their address with what they have stated in their application form. Now you can go to their house and wait to see if your partner arrives here. And all the above comes into play when you are doing your surveillance. I think that just about covers it for following your partner, you just have to be careful and make sure that you are not seen.

Do you have suspicions that your partner has been using your house to entertain their lover? This can be very distressing to find out especially if they have been using your bed, it can make you feel invaded and uncomfortable. In these circumstances, it is only likely to happen if you work, or are away for whatever reason and your partner is sure that you won't be home. If this is the case then you have to keep your eye out for anything that seems out of place. For example, there may be 2 wine glasses in the dishwasher or on the side. The bed is unmade and untidy. There may be a used condom packet in one of the bins or if smoking is allowed in the house, there may be another brand of cigarettes in the ashtray that you or your partner does not smoke. As you can see, most of these things are little, and cannot be questioned without proof.

So this is where you can spring your trap, tell your partner that in a weeks time you are spending a few days with your mum, family or friend who lives out of town. Its good to give them a week's notice because then they have the chance to let their lover know that your house will be free and can make plans. You have to make the story convincing by saying why you are going away, what you will be doing and that you are looking forward to it. It may be worth setting up a camera or recording device in the bedroom, but if you said you are going to be away for a weekend, then you may not catch anything on film, as nothing might happen till the 2nd night. Sometimes it can be best just to say you are going away for one night only, that way if anything does happen, then it will defiantly be on this night. Just make sure you say you won't be back until late afternoon the next day.

You do not have to sit and wait outside, but it may be a good idea to, so you know exactly what is going on and who may turn up to visit. If you do not want to wait then go to see a friend or something, it's up to you whether you tell them what you are doing or not, but you could even bring them back with you. It's not necessary, but it can be very embarrassing for you and your friend to walk in on your partner when they are doing the dirty on you. And it is also good to have someone there for support or in case it kick off, as these things do sometimes happen when people have been caught cheating. Now is the important bit, you have to plan your timing perfectly, because if you go back too early, then you could blow it. The last thing you want to do is blow it, because you won't get a chance to do this again. When you arrive back at the house, there are a few things you have to take note of. Firstly, are the downstairs or living room lights on? If so, then you may be a bit too early, because you want to catch them out in bed, and if they are downstairs then they could be fully clothed or your partner might still be on their own.

The fact that they may not be in the bedroom still may not be relevant and its up to you if you decide to walk in at this stage. After all they still need to do some explaining when you walk in on them with someone else. The second thing to look out for is if there is a car parked outside the house or on the drive that you have not seen before. This is a good sign that there is someone visiting. If the lights downstairs are out and the bedroom lights are on or off, then you will find that this is the best time to make your entrance. You have to be very quiet, as you do not want to alert your partner to your presence. So Try and open the door as quietly as possible, and do not slam the door behind you. You might not have keys to the front door, especially if you do not live with your partner, so you need to knock on the door and when your partner answers, push past and say something like "I forgot something, I have to go and get it."

Then you can walk into the bedroom and see if there is anyone sitting in the bed. See if your partner tries to stop you, you will then know something is up, because if they had nothing to hide then they wouldn't get in your way. You have to make sure that you push past as soon as the door opens, because if they see it's you they could close the door. Anyway, if you do have keys and have quiet stairs then use this to your advantage, by stepping on each step on the edge, so the ball of your feet does not touch it. If the stairs are creaky then run up as fast as you can, because its no good trying to sneak up when every step you make can be heard throughout the house. Take a deep breath and prepare yourself, because you may not like what you are about to see.

If there is someone else in bed with your partner, you have caught them red handed and there is nothing they can do to cover it up. From this point on it is up to you what you plan to do. However if your partner is alone and asleep, then maybe there was no cheating going on after all, just close the door quietly and leave. All the advice I have given here may not always be applicable to your situation, but there must be at least one thing here that can help you out in some way. In section 1 I mentioned stealth phones, now if your partner has one, then they won't be flashing it about. Try hunting for it, look everywhere, in their work or gym bag, in a coat pocket, in the drawers, in the car, anywhere that you would not expect to find it. They may actually be using an older phone that they say they do not use anymore, because they updated it with a newer model.

If there is an older phone lying around, turn it on, see if there is an old sim card and put it in. The answer could be staring you in the face, you just need to look for it. If you find a stealth phone or an old phone, look in all the message folders, look in the phone book and also check out the recent and received calls log. Take down all the numbers that seem out of the ordinary. Check them up with your partner's current phone and see if there are any numbers missing or are under a different name. If your partner is out, then you probably won't find a stealth phone, as this will be the time when they will have it with them, so try looking for it when they are in the bath or busy with something. This applies to checking all the numbers in their normal phone too. This is the time when they are most vulnerable and you should have enough time to find out everything you need. I hope this guide has been useful and you will be able to use the information given in this book to suit your situation. A lot of it is common sense, and you are perfectly able to try new things to try out if you think it will work.

PART SEVEN

MAKE A RELATIONSHIP WORK

I could not complete the book without adding this into it. After all you may find out that your relationship is missing something or are worried that you may lose the one you love. So I am now going to try what I can to highlight the best points in keeping yourself and your partner happy so you do not have to worry about cheating or even breaking up. So what is love? It is an emotion that we all feel for a particular person or thing, it drives us and makes us happy. Scientists say that love is a chemical reaction in our brain that causes euphoric feelings towards another person. Some say they fell in love at first sight, while others gradually build it up over time, when they grow fonder of someone. But what do we mean when we say we love someone? How can we explain it? The word "I love you" is just a saying and can be thrown around to gain advantage over someone else when you want to get your own way. So if it is only a word, then we have to connect the word with what it means personally to you. If you are in love with someone, then why do you love them? What is it about a person that makes you love them? Do you think that you love them enough to do anything for them, even die for them? It is a mysterious and wonderful thing, that can make us do all kinds of things, but do you love someone enough to spend the rest of your life with someone? Doing everything in your power to make them happy and not letting anyone or anything get in the way? Life throws many obstacles at us and tests our strengths and weaknesses, you have to know how to deal with them, and how to prevent them getting in the way of your true love. I am going to try my best to help out here, but it isn't going to be as in depth as some other books are. Just a general guide and a few points to take note of.

As we know a relationship goes through many different stages, you have the 'honeymoon period,' 'the serious relationship,' 'engagement,' marriage and finally parenthood. It's hard work to get through all the stages, but it is the meaning of life. We are born, we get married, we have children, and then we die. Our children will do the same and it will go on and on. Human life's sole purpose is to reproduce, it's as simple as that. If we stopped reproducing, the human race would eventually be phased out. In order to complete this cycle we must first meet someone. It isn't hard to do, there is a partner for everyone out there, you just have to find them. It's at this point when you have to decide what you want to do. Are you interested in a fling? Life long partner, or just a boyfriend/girlfriend. The first thing you do when you have met someone is talk and find all about each other and gradually start to connect. You both will be very excited and eager to hear what the other person has to say and you will point out what you both have in common and what you don't have in common. If you are both feeling comfortable you will then start seeing each other and will probably want to spend as much time together as possible. This is commonly known as the 'Honeymoon period.' It is not the holiday you both have when you get married, but it's the time when you have both first met and are very happy together. You will go out, introduce your friends and family, and the world will feel like its a million miles away and you are the only two people in the room.

This will not last forever, and alough it's a nice feeling to have at this stage, you will eventually break down into a routine. You will get to the point where you are no longer asking questions about your partner, because they have either told you or you have found out yourself. You will also know all there is to know about your partner and you will know if you want stay with them. You will also know if you don't see the relationship going anywhere and decide not to continue with it. You may have already had your first argument you may not, but if you have then you will want to patch it up as soon as possible. An argument this early into the relationship will also tell you what their temperament is like. This is a good time to break down the personality of your partner. Decide whether the argument was trivial, an accident or serious. If the argument was over something as silly as forgetting to call your partner back when you said you would, then you will know that they may be the sort of person that starts arguments quite easily. You will then think "well if he/she went off over something like that then, what will it be like if we have a proper argument?" It is not necessary to start worrying about this too much as it is still too early in the relationship, and it might be the case that they were just having a bad day and you caught the back of it.

If the argument was over an accident or a misunderstanding, then it will pretty much sort itself out, after all you are both in the 'honeymoon period' and you do not want to argue over something when it can be easily forgotten.

If it was a serious argument this early in the relationship, depending on what it was, you may be in trouble. Some relationships were just not meant to be, and you can both split up before you have really started. You may talk it through and patch things up, but you must recognise what the problem was and learn from it so you do not cause it to happen again. Any general argument can be sorted out, you both have to make the effort and communicate properly and find out what your needs are. It's easy to give up and move on, so many people do it, that's why there are so many divorces today. If you are spending too much time out with your friends and it is causing a strain on your relationship, then compromise, you can go out less or take your partner with you. If you work unsociable hours, then try to make a point of explaining that you can't help it, you have to work to get money. If its possible to change your hours at work then make the effort, it's not all that hard. If you are a smoker and you partner isn't and they don't like smoking, you don't necessarily have to quit, you can try to cut down or make the effort not to smoke in front of them. Can you see the picture I am trying to lay down here? It's all about compromise and communication, if you sort a problem out before it becomes a big issue, then you have nothing to worry about.

After the 'honeymoon period,' you then notice that you are both happily settled together and move into a routine. You no longer introduce your partner as "My new boyfriend/girlfriend" you will just be the boyfriend or the girlfriend. You will probably calm things down a bit now, and you won't always be over each other, constantly kissing and being together as much as before. Alough these changes are quite big, they will make you stronger. Everybody needs to have their space, its unhealthy to be attached by the waist all the time, and you don't want to tire the relationship out, so you settle down and carry on with your life as you did while you were single, with the bonus of now having a partner to share it with. You will find that at this stage you will gain trust and security, where this was being built up in the 'honeymoon period.' After all the 'honeymoon period' will last a month maybe two, and in this time you will be gaining security by being all over your partner showing them how much you want them, and finding out what sort of person they are and if you can trust them.

When you have reached the 'serious relationship' stage, you will know them inside out and you don't need to prove you aren't going to leave them by clinging on to them all the time. If you have both made it this far then you are looking at a long-term relationship, unless fate suggests otherwise. Many people have suffered the blindness of love virus. I should know, it has happened to me enough times. If you have heard the phrase "love is blind" then it will refer to someone who was too much in love with their partner that they can never see the bad points and will not listen to anyone who says anything bad about them.

This is a psychological thing, because as far as you are concerned there is nothing wrong with your partner, if they treat you bad or have a tendency to upset your friends, you will disregard the negative parts from your brain and not step back and look at things rationally.

By the time you actually open your eyes and see the bad points of your partner, you have usually already split up, so it's a good thing to try and keep your eyes open to the fact that nobody is perfect and everybody has negative points. If your friends can see them, then you should defiantly see them. If the negative side of your partner becomes a problem in the relationship, you must try to fix it as soon as possible. The reason for this is, if you don't say anything, then they won't know there is a problem, and after a while it will be harder to sort out. Once you have identified all your partner's bad points, you then have to work out what their good points are. See how many good and how many bad. You may be in trouble if you come out with more bad than good, because relationships are not held together on negativity. Here is an example of some of mine. These are based on what I have been told and not what I personally think.

Good Points

1. Funny
2. Caring
3. Loving
4. Generous
5. Puts others first
6. Crazy
7. Strong willed
8. Good personality

9. Ambitious
10. Protective

Bad Points

1. Sometimes does not listen or forgets easy
2. Says the wrong things at the wrong time
3. With your friends too much
4. Do not always show your real feelings

These are just some points I can remember, but it is harder to try and read yourself than reading someone else. You shouldn't worry about the good points, as these are the positive things that make your relationship work. You only need to concentrate on the negative points. For instance, I have been told that I do not always show my real feelings. I have talked about this with my partner and explained that I can sometimes get shy to show my feelings or embarrassed, not to mention I have been hurt a few times in the past so keeping them locked up keeps me safe from getting hurt again. After I explained this, my partner was more understanding about it and not paranoid that I had no feelings at all. We came to a compromise that if I made a bit more of an effort to show my feelings, then she would not pester me about it all the time. I have also talked about when I don't listen or when I forget things, I explained that I sometimes have a short attention span and if someone is trying to talk to me when I am watching the TV, then my mind is concentrated on one thing and everything else is blocked out.

I think this is more of a man's thing than a woman's because it is a proven fact that women listen more than men. Women are also more likely to show their feelings than men, because women tend to be more loving and caring and generally are not embarrassed to show it. You will notice that there are a lot of significant differences between man and woman. It is nothing new, or modern, most of these differences go way back to caveman times. The human race is really no different from animals, as each species have their own animal behaviour, which includes humans too. For example, 10,000 years ago, when we were living in caves. The man would be the dominant hunter, going out to find food and bring it back to the cave. The female would be the submissive mother, staying in the cave looking after the children.

Now due to the many years mankind has evolved and with our modern society, we can easily argue that we are all different from our Neanderthal ancestors. I argue that there are still many similarities between now and 10,000 years ago. Firstly, the man is commonly accepted as the provider of the family. He will go out to work and earn money to put food on the table and clothes on his children. This is the same basic concept as going out with a spear and hunting, as money was non-existent all those years ago. Women nowadays are treated equally as men and work the same jobs, but still stay at home and look after the children, when they are born, relying on the man to do the work for her. The only major changes we have seen over time are our individual personalities and the fact we can think for ourselves. We communicate clearer than before and we can tell the difference between right and wrong. Nowadays if you were to live in a cave and run around with a spear in your hand, you are likely to get arrested for carrying a dangerous weapon and killing some farmers live stock. Without going too far off track, the point I am trying to make is that we have more problems with our relationships now than we used to, because of how we communicate and how our individual personalities work in modern society. Our world is quite interesting now, because we have submissive men, dominant women, homosexuality is acceptable and we live and dress the way we want.

When you are at the 'serious relationship' stage, you will probably want to start up a home together. On occasion you may decide that it is too soon, due to money reasons, or the fact that you are happy as you are for the moment, but usually if you have been together for a while then this usually becomes an option. You need to sit down and talk about it, and decide if it is what you both want and what you are looking for in a home. Do not rush into it, especially if you haven't been together for long, because going out with someone is a different world to actually living with them. There is a lot more work involved in keeping the house tidy, decorated and also being able to afford one. You will also be together 24 hours a day 7 days a week, and if you are someone who likes to have space, then you need to figure out how you can get it without finding it a problem.

It may be well and good if your partner works different hours to you, because you will have your own time, however if you both work different hours, then it could be a problem that you hardly get to see each other at all. You have to make a fine line between spending too much time together and not seeing each other at all, as this will put a strain on your relationship. You both need to be certain that you want to move in and that your relationship is strong enough to last. It is so hard to deal with if you have moved in and after a while you split up and one of you has to move out. If you think that everything is going to be fine and you are happy you're your decision then make sure you have a lot of money saved, you will see how quickly it goes after you get somewhere to live. As you are now living together, if you haven't noticed them before you will notice them now and that is bad habits.

Bad habits are a bit like bad points, which I mentioned earlier, but are not categorized in the same section. Bad points are mental and bad habits are physical. For example, you may be a smoker, burp too often, chew your toenails or leave the toilet seat up.

You can still work these out if you talk about them, for instance, not smoking in the house, putting the toilet seat down after you've used it and try not to burp as much. Sometimes it can be beneficial to go on holiday with your partner before you move in, because you will stay together all the time when you are away and this will temporarily give you an idea of what life is like living together. Some people claim that when they live together, their sex life starts to slow down, even to a stop. Now when I was living with my ex fiancée, I noticed this as well. It would be a case that she was too tired or wasn't in the mood. Living together can be hard work, as I have already stated. Washing up, making dinner, ironing complete with your day job as well, it can tire you out. You will also find that when you first move in together you will be having sex quite a lot, even doing it in every room of the new home. It may be great to have an active sex life when you live together, but it can start to decrease after a while, so you have to make sure you do not over do it. You could later find that it becomes a chore or get boring doing the same thing over and over again. Try not to have sex every night and every morning. If you have come to the point where you feel sex is boring, then try new things.

There is a wide range of things you can do, like trying new positions for a start. Buy a book called the 'Kama Sutra.' The Kama Sutra of Vatsyayana ("Kama Sutra" is Sanskrit for "Aphorisms of Love") is an extraordinary and fascinating work that deserves careful reading and study. Written in ancient India, it is essentially a technical guide, a scholarly treatise if you will, to sexual enjoyment and other sensual pleasures. It also contains profound historical and anthropological insights into the mores and customs of ancient India. The modern reader will often be surprised by how markedly different the cultural paradigms presented in the Kama Sutra are from those of today. Almost nothing is known about the writer, Vatsyayana, or the exact date he wrote this work. Regarding the date, Sir Richard F. Burton translated the Kama Sutra in 1883, from this he determined from internal evidence that the Kama Sutra was written sometime between the first and sixth centuries A.D. Many scholars now believe the Kama Sutra was written during, or shortly before, the Gupta period (320-540 A.D.), which has also been called the Classical Age of India. Regarding the writer

Vatsyayana, Burton makes the following insightful remarks:

"...He [Vatsyayana] states that he wrote the work while leading the life of a religious student (probably at Benares) and while wholly engaged in the contemplation of the Deity. He must have arrived at a certain age at that time, for throughout he gives us the benefit of his experience, and of his opinions, and these bear the stamp of age rather than of youth; indeed the work could hardly have been written by a young man." One comment should be made about the so-called "Kama Sutra" now available at various sites on the Internet. That text document, the so-called "sexual positions list" is only a very small snippet of the entire work (a portion of one chapter out of a total of 35 chapters plus a Salutation.) It is also not from the Burton translation. The whole scholarly (and some would say, practical) character of the Kama Sutra is nothing like most works of erotica written today. Some would even assert that the Kama Sutra is wholly appropriate even for older teens to read because of its historical and anthropological insights into our own culture and to human sexuality in general. Of course, our society is a lot different from ancient Indian society. Thus, many of the subjects and cultural practices Vatsyayana discusses are very alien, and even bizarre, to our frame of reference. But that is what makes the Kama Sutra so fascinating, something written almost two millennia ago, in a culture far removed us, tells us today that there is more than one way for a society to regulate human sexual practice and conduct. Many people have praised the book due to its graphic images and unusual sexual positions, proving that there are so many ways to reach sexual ecstasy other than the more common positions we use all the time. It will take a long while to try all of the positions described and illustrated in the book, but you will both agree that there are some that will make your sex life better. You can find details about the Kama Sutra in the next chapter, along with many other useful books. It may be the case that sex itself has become boring no matter what position you try. So you need to take a look at other options that will suit you better. After all sex isn't just restricted to intercourse. You could try role-playing, which to some may seem silly and embarrassing, but unless you have actually tried it, you cannot really judge it. For example you may have a very big crush on 'Lara Croft' from the popular 'Tomb Raider' games, so would it not be fun to get your girlfriend to dress up as 'Lara Croft,' and you can imagine you are actually having sex with her. Now this only works if your partner agrees to do it and isn't jealous of the fact that you want to have sex with a computer generated computer game character. But if you both love and trust each other then there shouldn't be a problem. After all you may want your boyfriend to dress up as a fireman or even superman, its all whatever takes your fancy. Don't be afraid, nobody else is going to see you, and if it makes the sex better then its all for the good of your relationship.

Some people even dress up and play act with scripts, like I said it may seem childish, but its all fun and it opens you mind to your fantasies. If role-playing isn't your thing, then maybe a bit of domination and trying something kinky may work. You will obviously know who the dominant one out of you both is. Hopefully you both know what you are doing and have the proper respect for each other and keep it safe, there is nothing wrong with a bit of pain. Light spanking, pulling of hair, candle wax on the body that sort of thing. So long as it isn't dangerous and your partner is happy to do the things you want to do. Some couples have problems in their sex life because their partner refuses to give oral or anal, after all, due to personal opinion, those sorts of things may not appeal to them. You just have to compromise and not try to force them to do anything they don't want to do. In some cases, it is this sort of thing that causes people to become unfaithful to their partner. They either don't get what they want in bed and look for it elsewhere or there is no sex at all in the relationship.

You have to make sure that you are aware that a serious relationship is based on more than just sex, otherwise you are not a couple, you are just two people who have sex. If you feel that you are being pressured into doing something you don't want to do sexually, please don't feel you have to do it, because it is more fun if you enjoy it rather than being forced to do it. And do not fall for the old saying "If you love me then you will do it."

This is emotional black mail. The only answer to that is "Okay, if you love me then you won't force me to do it." There may be a lot of sexual acts that you find disgusting or you don't want to do, but you should at least try it first and you could be surprised that it might not have been as bad as you thought it was. If you still don't like it after trying it then tell your partner, at least you made the effort to have a go. Then you can try and think of something you want to do to them, everyone has a fantasy, and you will more than likely get them to do it because after all, you did something for them that you may not of been happy about doing, so its only fair that you do something you want to do back.

Some people like voyeurism or having a threesome. Now unlike cheating, this is something that is consented by both parties. Voyeurism is where you like to watch someone having sex with your partner and you do not get involved in any form of sexual contact. Or you may like to try having a threesome. Be it two men and one woman or two women and one man. I would like to advise a lot of caution with doing this, as it can make or break a relationship. Especially if you prefer the sex with the other person, you could end up falling out or breaking up completely.

Not everybody wants to have a threesome, because at the end of the day, there are only 2 people in a relationship and most people do not want to share you with someone else. Not to mention it is not always the easiest thing to arrange, especially as you need to find the 3rd person who will also be willing to join in. Before you even consider anything like this, you and your partner have to be 100% sure that you love and trust each other enough to actually go through with it. It will play big time on your relationship afterwards. You both must have a good understanding and come to an agreement that it will not damage the love you have for each other. If you are both satisfied that you both are happy to do it and you won't have problems afterwards, make sure you play safe, whether or not you use protection with yourselves as a couple, you must make sure you use it when you bring in another person. Good sex is safe sex that's all I can say. There is no point agreeing that you will both be fine after you have a threesome and you later find out you have contracted a sexually transmitted disease, because believe it or not, this will cause problems, especially if you have to go to the VD clinic and explain how you got it.

I found that it can be quite a turn on if you film it with a video camera, you can then sit back and watch it with your partner and become aroused by watching yourselves having sex.

A lot of the time your partner could be worried about filming it in case you decide it would be fun to show your mates or use it against them if you split up, so a lot of trust and care must be taken if you want to make an erotic home video.

These are just a few things to start you off, there are many more things out there, you just have to open your mind. Nothing is perverted, it only becomes apparent that a particular sexual act is perverted when someone says it is, so do not worry. Try to live out your sexual fantasies, everybody has them.

While you both have spent a while in the 'serious relationship' stage, it will eventually move on to the 'engagement' stage. When you reach the point where you or your partner has proposed and it's been accepted, you will now know that whatever the odds, you are hoping to spend the rest of your lives together. For some people, engagement can seem like a daunting experience, because they will never get the chance to be with anyone else, (unless they decide to cheat) but with this in mind, if you truly love your partner, then you won't want to be with anyone else. Engagement can last years, depending on money or your personal situation, or it can last months. When you become engaged to someone, you are usually already living with them, so you should know very well that married life will be no different from being a live in lover.

If you do not live together when you get engaged, you will have to find somewhere to live, and as I have mentioned earlier, houses do not come cheap. You will find that buying or renting a house on top of getting married will cost an absolute fortune. The average church wedding will cost you around about £20,000. It is advisable that before you make any definite wedding plans, you make sure your house is all set up and you are financially stable to continue. There is nothing worse than being broke before you have even started your life together, I have been there myself and it is not a nice thing to happen.

You will find that the women are the ones who do most of the wedding arrangements, as this is something they have planned since they were children. All women dream about their wedding day and want it to be perfect. So try not to interfere with it too much unless it sounds a bit more than you can afford, when you could easily cut down on a few small things. If you want to get involved with the wedding, just ask, I'm sure she won't mind, just don't expect her to let you pick out the bridal dress, because this is something she will want, and its bad luck for a man to see the dress before the wedding. The plus side of course is that you both get to arrange your stag and hen nights, however you decide to have them is entirely up to you. Men's stag nights usually consist of going out with all the boys, getting seriously drunk and having a stripper do a dance for you. The old tradition of waking up tied to a lamp post while stripped half naked are pretty rare but do still happen, depending on how wild your friends are. Female hen nights are usually the same, but in a generally more sensible setting. It may be a good idea not to have your stag/hen party, the night before your wedding. This is tradition, but it isn't nice to have your big day, when you are hung over or painted pink by a party member the evening before. You may think that getting drunk isn't the thing for you. A lot of people choose to have a day out playing paintball, or go carting. Some even decide to have a lost weekend in Amsterdam, and I probably do not need to go into detail on what happens there. Just make sure you have enough time to get home, and your bride to be is perfectly ok with you to spend a drunken weekend in the sexual capital of Europe.

I'm sure you are aware that the next step is going to obviously be 'Marriage' and this is the point where you are joined together in a legal contract as husband and wife. The day has come, you have you home sorted out and you have the money to pay for your big day. A lot of people suffer from cold feet, and start to panic. The reality of marriage has set in and can start to play with your mind. Have we rushed this? Do I want to be with one person for the rest of my life? Will I be a bad husband/wife? It will all be swimming through your mind, clouding your judgement. Let it pass and do not let it swallow you up, you had you chance to say no when the proposal was first made, and now it is the point of no return. If you walk away now you won't get the same chance with your partner again. He/she will more than likely finish you on the spot, and his/her friends and family will not take lightly to it either. Ok you have said your wedding vowels, signed your marriage certificate, had a lot to drink at your reception, and come home from your honeymoon. You now start your life together as a married couple.

You will probably see that married life is no different than just being in a relationship, except you now have a ring and a piece of paper saying its official. You should both feel very happy and nothing on the planet will break you apart. Unfortunately, people still break apart all the time, and have to go through divorce, which will involve the courts, and a lot of heartache. The way I see it, divorce should be an absolute last resort. Make sure that whatever problems you may come across are sorted out. Do not give up, until all options are exhausted, this will include, talking about the problem, making an effort to correct the problem, even going to see a marriage councillor and get advice from them.

So why do people have more problems in marriage, than in a simple relationship?

For one, it can be that you both have started to grow apart, you are in debt, have children problems or are just not happy anymore. There shouldn't be any difference in how you sort your problems now than you did when you only just met. Unless it is the same problem that just won't go away. For example you may have drank too much when you were going out, and now you drink the same or even more than at first. If the original problem when you first met is still ongoing, you have to sort it out, or you can have disastrous consequences. There is always a solution to every problem. If you are an alcoholic, you can see alcohol anonymous, if it's a drug related problem, you can see your doctor and he could help out and arrange rehab. You may find that domestic violence has become a problem. I do not condone this sort of thing, and firmly believe that if you have a lot of problems going on in your life, you shouldn't take them out on your wife and children, as it solves nothing. It hurts them more than you think. If you are a victim of domestic violence, and you feel that you are trapped, there are people who can help. Doing nothing will not solve it, but make it worse over time. It saddens me to hear this, but some women who suffer domestic violence, do not leave their husbands due to fear, or the fact that they love them too much and they say, "he doesn't really mean it, he does love me too, but he has a lot on his mind." Nothing can be that bad that you have to lash out and physically hurt the one you love. Taking your anger out on your family is cowardly and cruel. There is no excuse for it. You could be looking at a criminal prosecution that will entail a fine, restraining order, or maybe even a custodial sentence. If you end up getting sent to prison, you will find that your life will be a lot worse than it was before. You both have to seek help immediately, if you feel that domestic violence is starting to take over your life.

If you feel you are a victim of domestic violence, there are many options available to you, consult your doctor, he will have a wealth of information to help you out and can point you in the right direction. He will also give you information on organizations that can help, or you can visit http://www.womensaid.org.uk/ this is a website made for women who need help with domestic violence. You are not alone, and you must not feel isolated, you cannot keep quiet and do nothing, you have a right to be happy without the fear of having a violent husband. This goes for your children too, sometimes they can be caught up in domestic violence and it can have a lot of physical and mental effects on them as they grow up. Especially if they believe that it is acceptable to be violent as they have been brought up with it and see it as being normal.

Moving away from this subject now, we can now concentrate briefly on the sex life problems. I have covered a lot of this in the 'serious relationship' stage. There is nothing new to suggest here as the same things apply as before. Just remember to communicate and try new things. You should not have a non-existent sex life due to marriage.

You will find that the biggest problem everyone has in life usually has something to do with money. We live in a buy it now, pay later society, where people are keen to buy things with a credit card and worry about the repayments later. With this in mind, you will find that you can get into debt very easily, and it's hard to get out after a certain point. Debts can cause people to suffer from depression or even suicide, so you have to be aware of all your income and outgoing bills. If you realise that a new car is too much to afford, then wait. If you struggle with the repayments you could be looking at it getting repossessed and gaining a bad credit rating. If your money trouble is getting you depressed there are still people who can help. Have a word with your local citizens advice office and see how you stand at getting the problem sorted. You could be looking at going bankrupt, it will give you a bad credit rating and you will not be able to register a business in your own name, but your debts will be wiped clean.

Going bankrupt isn't as bad as it used to be, it can help your situation if you find there is no other alternative. Usually the best thing to do is try to get a loan that will take care of all your debts so you only have one payment. Try to seek help from a financial adviser and they can tell you your best options available. Try to use a loan company that have a low APR and try not to pay back the loan with the minimum payment's as you will find you are paying more interest. If you find you have a bit more money due to saving or cutting down on monthly spending try to pay your loan off a bit quicker. Do not use a loan shark, as most are not registered and have very high interest rates. Some can get nasty if you fail to pay back what they ask, so its better to use an official organization that can survive not being paid back.

Married life can put a big strain on you both, with money or the day-to-day chores of looking after your house and keeping your partner happy. At some point you may want to complicate your life a bit more and have kids. In our modern way of life, people tend to have kids before getting married or even engaged. The moral opinion of having sex before marriage is pretty much in the past. The sad thing is teenagers are having children as young as 12 and alough this shocking fact may surprise a lot of people, it has come a way of life. Either way, if you are married or still in a relationship, and children are what you want, you have to be prepared. Children are more expensive than anything you have ever bought before, and they will cost you lots of money up to the point where they want their own independence. This can be from 16 to 21, either way you are looking at being very poor for a long time. If you are planning for children or they come by accident, which is quite common, the first thing you have to do is start buying baby stuff. You have a lot to consider as babies are very demanding and need a lot of things. To mention a few, you need to look at buying the following things,

Clothes
Pram/Buggy
Cot
Feeding accessories
High chair
Nappies and changing accessories
Creams and shampoos
Baby food
Car seat

The list goes on, and Cots and prams can cost up to £300 each. So before the child is even born, you will have already spent a fortune on it. Parenthood will be the final stage you go through, until your children grow up and leave home. By this time you will be older, wiser and preparing for retirement, depending on your age when you become parents. It is usually best to wait until you can afford them before actually having them, so don't feel that you must rush into having them. If you are unprepared for them and they come naturally you will have to make do with your situation and talk about cutting costs and saving. You will have a new priority and kids always come first before your own needs. This shouldn't mean that it would come between your relationship or marriage, as you have to still make time for that as well. With the increase on taxes and inflation, you have to be aware of costs at all times. If you are having money or debt problems, try to get them sorted as soon as possible, you cannot afford to be in debt with a newborn baby on the way. Most new parents worry that they might mess it up or not know what to do when the baby is born. It's perfectly normal to worry, as you all want to be good parents. It will all come naturally and you will be the happiest people on earth when you hold your child for the first time. Having kids can put a strain on your marriage, because they are dependant on you day and night and you have to be able to provide their needs. They will tire you out, as most kids around 2-5 are a nightmare. They are full of energy and crave attention, you have to make sure that you know the difference between giving them what they want and spoiling them.

Don't get me wrong, spoiling your children from time to time is good, but if they begin to expect everything they want instead of ask for it, you will not get the proper respect as a parent. Spoiling children can also have a lot of psychological effects when they grow up, because they will not grow out of it, they will become more needy when they reach their teens, as it becomes harder on them to gain independence when they think other people will do everything for them. I can relate this very well because when I was younger my mother spoilt me rotten and did everything for me. By the time I reached my late teens, having everything done for me instead of doing it myself seemed like the normal way of life, and I wish that my mum had been harder on me when I was younger so I could learn to do things for myself, instead of getting her to do them for me.

Giving your children the correct discipline should be carefully looked at as well. As I have said, kids can be very trying and very often make you mad, but keeping self-control over the situation at hand is a must. There is a line between punishing you kids and beating them senseless. Smacking is a very controversial matter that many do not approve of, yet others think it's the only way. Now I do not want to get into the subject of what is right or wrong, as it is more or less down to the parents themselves who decide if they want to smack their kids.

If your child is misbehaving, then you should step in immediately and tell them to stop it. Say it in a firm but not a loud voice. You have to show them the difference between right and wrong at a young age so they know when they are not allowed to do something or know that they will get told off for it. So say for instance your son/daughter is throwing a ball inside the house and it is getting too close to your prize ornaments. Stand up and say "No, stop doing that in the house you are going to break something." You have then told them off and explained to them why you have told them off. If they continue you can step in and say "I have told you once and I will tell you one more time, stop throwing your ball about or I will take it off of you." Generally this will work, as they don't want their toys taken away from them. The problem is that young kids have a short attention span, and will sometimes carry on doing it again after a while. If they continue to throw the ball around you can then take the ball away from them and hide it. You are more than likely going to get a tantrum kick off after this, or just maybe the child will start crying. You have to tell them why you took the ball off of them, and they will remember that you warned them. Kids are not as stupid as people make them out to be, they are aware of what is going on, and when a threat is made like the warning of having the ball taken away, if it is then carried out, your children will quickly learn that if you say you are going to do something, you will actually do it.This may act as a deterrent in future, so for instance if your kids are playing up, and you have told them off but they do not listen, you can impose the ultimatum, "If you do not behave I will smack your bottom, or you will not get any sweets today." If you have stuck by your words before then they will know that you will stick by them now. The threat of getting a smack can usually get a child to behave. If you don't believe in smacking I would not advice warning them that you will, because if you say you will smack them and you do not when they carry on misbehaving, then you have shown a weakness in the fact that your threats won't be carried out and they can continue misbehaving. You can try to use the warning with a raised voice, not necessarily shouting, but not firm, a raised voice shows authority and children tend to step back and take note of it. A good form of punishment is to make them sit on the naughty step or the naughty corner. A very simple technique where you make them sit on one of the stairs or a corner for 20 minutes and not move or say anything. For a toddler, sitting down and keeping quiet is a very hard thing to do, so if you make them do it and tell them to think about what they have done. In most cases 20 minutes will feel like forever and they will generally think that maybe writing on the wall was a bad thing and not something they will want to do again.

Of course this method won't work when they get to a particular age, usually around 6 upwards, so you have to try a new method. Turning off the TV or saying that if they are going to be naughty, then they can't watch their favourite programme is effective, or just sending them to their room for the rest of the night. So long as they do not have anything to keep themselves busy like a TV or play station. If you take these out, then they will have nothing to do but sit bored and think, and this is what we want them to do. You can give them a book to read, which is good for their learning development, and the fact that most children nowadays hardly even read a book, because they have too much to do with computers and DVDs. It is unhealthy for them to be constantly watching TV or playing computer games, they need to get out or read a book every now and again.

You shouldn't give your children too many sweets or fatty meals, but if they have been good then the odd McDonalds here and a chocolate bar there won't do any harm. Especially if they know they have been awarded it for good behaviour, it encourages them to stay good for most of the time. When your kids start to get to their teens, you will find that they will want to go out more and socialise with their friends, so obviously the punishment here would be to ground them if they are playing up. I have noticed that kids as young as 6 carry mobile phones, but to be honest I do not think kids should own a mobile phone until they are old enough or responsible enough to use them.

If you are going to ground your teenage kids, then make sure they have no access to their phone as well, so you are pretty much cutting them off from their friends. They will not like this and will kick up a stink about it, but they must learn that if they do something wrong, they have to be punished. The teenager stage for a parent is probably going to be the hardest, because they get to the age where they are more likely to answer back and try to defy your rules. You should always still remain on top and do not let them walk over you, because if you let them get away with their behaviour, then they will not respect you and will have no regard for your rules. It is a known fact by government statistics that teenagers who are unruly and cause havoc in the streets come from broken homes. They have no respect for other people or property and I say that somewhere down the line, it is the parents that have not given the proper discipline or upbringing, to teach them the respect that they have to give. Not all kids who come from broken homes turn to crime and unsocial behaviour, but those that do, probably have not been given the correct attention for when they do right and wrong. I don't want to go too deeply into this subject, as it can be debatable for many people reading this that it might not necessarily be true, but generally the matter of anti social teenagers is ongoing and they come from all kinds of living situations.

After you kids have grown up and left home, they have more than likely started a relationship with someone themselves, and you can happily see the cycle that you and your partner start all over again. You will probably find it quite amusing when they are having girlfriend/boyfriend problems and when you step in to help they can come out with something like "I don't want to tell you, because your old and won't understand." The reason why this is amusing is because we have all been there, done it and bought the T-shirt. There is nothing your kids won't go through which you probably haven't already gone through yourself. It won't hurt to offer a little relationship advice, but sometimes it can be best for them to find out on their own and learn from their mistakes. People and times change, but the same problems stick around from generation to generation, there is nothing new that hasn't already happened before. We get older, and we get wiser, the older we get the more helpful we become to our kids and others around us. Someone said that we keep learning right up to the day we die, and if it doesn't kill us, it can only make us stronger.

That has covered as much as I can think of for this book, and I am hoping that you have found it useful for whatever your problem may be. I have taken a long time and a lot of effort into putting this book together and nearly all of what is written is based on personal experience and common facts. I do hope that there is someone who has read this and afterwards it has made a difference to their relationship in some way. I am hoping to start a new project on another book soon, so hopefully I will make that a success too. Thank you for buying this book, and remember to look after those who love you, it is the meaning of life, to grow up, fall in love and die happy.

PART EIGHT

USEFUL BOOKS & LINKS

If the advice in this book has helped you in what you need to do, but you still need a bit more, then I will add a whole list of useful websites, and books that will make things even easier for you. Some of the below can be used for both sections of this book so have a read if you think they will help.

www.Amazon.co.uk - An online bookshop that is very useful and a good start to find what you need.

http://www.womensaid.org.uk/ - A website made to help women who are trapped by domestic violence.

www.Ebay.co.uk - Very addictive and very useful. An auction website, where you can buy or sell anything, you will find things on here you would never even think of. Also a great source for books and guides.

www.Faceparty.com - A friends/dating website that is great if you want to meet new people, or if you think your partner has a profile on here.

www.Lycos.co.uk - Click on Love @ Lycos and you will get a very popular dating website, as with face party.

www.loopylove.co.uk - Another popular online dating site.

The Definitive book of body language – a useful book on detecting liars, or if people may feel attracted to you. Found in any large bookshop or Amazon.

I know what you're really thinking: Reading body language like a Trial Lawyer – Another useful book on body language, found on Amazon and other good book shops.

Lies: And the people who tell them: A book on lying, how to find out. Found on Amazon and other good shops.

The UK book of Post Codes – A book with every postcode listed, very useful if you need to find the town of someone who you think is seeing your partner. Found in any British post office.

Private investigators handbook – This is the book that will help you become a successful private investigator, but be aware, you need to be fully qualified with certificate, if you plan to start a business. The course can cost a lot of money, so if you need to use a more in depth guide on following someone or finding a cheating partner, then it can be quite handy. Found on Ebay.

Women are from Venus, Men are From Mars – A famous and yet very useful book to read. All about relationships and why men and women are so different. If you find you are having problems with your relationship, or you need the confidence to meet that special person, then have a good read. Found on Amazon, and any bookshop.

Kama Sutra – A very popular book, made thousands of years ago, showing graphic images of sexual acts and a guide on how to enhance your sex life.

About The Author

David Roger Jones, 24 years old and born and bred in Hertfordshire UK. I learnt most of my cheating tricks in my early 20's when I was stuck in a relationship I could not get out of. I was with a girl who would not take no for an answer if I tried to dump her and every time I tried to bring it up, she would always find a way to change the subject. She was very jealous and paranoid, had low self-esteem and lived for me. After a year of being with her, I felt trapped, I no longer wanted to be with her, but was worried what she would do if I split up with her. In the end I decided to see other people, and find my happiness elsewhere. I started to learn some new tricks on how to become undetectable, and also the things that nearly caught me out I would learn from, and use so they would never happen again. I can't say that I know everything, because you are always learning new things all the time, but as we learn, we get better at what we do.

I just want to help those who need assistance in cheating and learn not to make the same mistakes I made, or if you need to find out if you have been cheated on, how to go about finding out. I have stopped cheating now, as I have found the love of my life, and she helped me see my responsibilities and that there is more to life than having a fling. I do wish that life and relationships were so easy, but it's a hard world to live in and relationships will test everyone on love, trust and their happiness. I have done a lot of things in my life that I am not proud of, and cheating is one of them. A friend as a joke told me that I should write a book about how to cheat, and this made my mind tingle. Since then I have tried to put as much effort into this book as possible and make it useful to anyone that needs help. I have written short stories before and like all books you read, it inspires your mind, however I wanted to write a book that not only inspires, but also guides others. You may think you do not need this book, because your relationship is solid, but I can tell you now, that no relationship is 100% solid. They could be cheating on you right now, you might not even know about it. But I'm sure you would like to have the comfort in knowing what signs to look for and what might be going wrong in your relationship in order for them to cheat. I hope that everyone who reads this will put it to good use one way or another.